I0448831

AUG. 24, 2005

Third Status Report to the Attorney General on Body Armor Safety Initiative Testing and Activities

NCJ 210418

Sarah V. Hart
Director

Cover photograph of law enforcement officer by Larry Levine, courtesy of the Washington Metropolitan Area Transit Authority, 2001.

The National Institute of Justice is a component of the Office of Justice Programs, which also includes the Bureau of Justice Assistance, the Bureau of Justice Statistics, the Office of Juvenile Justice and Delinquency Prevention, and the Office for Victims of Crime.

U.S. Department of Justice
Office of Justice Programs
National Institute of Justice

Third Status Report to the Attorney General on
Body Armor Safety Initiative
Testing and Activities

Table of Contents

U.S. Department of Justice
Office of Justice Programs
National Institute of Justice

Third Status Report to the Attorney General on
Body Armor Safety Initiative
Testing and Activities

Executive Summary

On November 17, 2003, Attorney General John Ashcroft announced the U.S. Department of Justice's Body Armor Safety Initiative in response to concerns from the law enforcement community regarding the effectiveness of body armor in use. These concerns followed the failure of a relatively new Zylon®-based[1] body armor vest worn by a Forest Hills, Pennsylvania, police officer. The Attorney General directed the National Institute of Justice (NIJ) to initiate an examination of Zylon®-based bullet-resistant armor (both new and used), to analyze upgrade kits provided by manufacturers to retrofit Zylon®-based bullet-resistant armors, and to review the existing program by which bullet-resistant armor is tested to determine if the process needs modification.

As part of the Body Armor Safety Initiative, NIJ has issued two status reports to the Attorney General containing results from the body armor studies.[2] The first two status reports highlighted the following findings:

- Ballistic-resistant material, including Zylon®, can degrade due to environmental factors, thus reducing the ballistic resistance safety margin that manufacturers build into their armor designs.
- The ultimate tensile strength[3] of single yarns removed from the rear panel of the Forest Hills armor was up to 30-percent lower than that of yarns from "new" armor supplied by the manufacturer. Artificially-aged armor of the same type that failed in the Forest Hills incident was ballistically tested, but no bullet penetrations occurred.[4]
- The upgrade kits tested did not appear to bring used armor up to the level of performance of new armor. However, used armors with upgrade kits performed better than the used armors alone.

NIJ has now completed ballistic and mechanical properties testing on 103 used Zylon®-containing body armors provided by law enforcement agencies across the United States. Sixty of these used armors (58%) were penetrated by at least one round during a six-shot test series. Of the armors that were not penetrated, 91% had backface deformations in excess of that allowed by

---

[1] Zylon® (PBO fiber – poly-*p*-phenylene benzobisoxazole) is a high-strength organic fiber produced by Toyobo Co., Ltd. Zylon® is a registered trademark of Toyobo Co., Ltd.

[2] "Status Report to the Attorney General on Body Armor Safety Initiative Testing and Activities," March 11, 2004, and "Supplement I: Status Report to the Attorney General on Body Armor Safety Initiative Testing and Activities," December 27, 2004.

[3] Ultimate tensile strength is the maximum stress (force per unit area) that a material, in this case a Zylon® yarn, can withstand prior to failure. All Zylon® yarns were nominally 500 denier; *i.e.*, the yarns did not vary in linear density or effective cross-sectional area.

[4] NIJ continues to study the Forest Hills body armor penetration, to resolve the cause of that failure.

U.S. Department of Justice
Office of Justice Programs
National Institute of Justice

Third Status Report to the Attorney General on
Body Armor Safety Initiative
Testing and Activities

the NIJ standard for new armor. Only four of the used Zylon®-containing armors met all performance criteria expected under the NIJ standard for new body armor compliance.

Although these results do not conclusively prove that all Zylon®-containing body armor models have performance problems, the results clearly show that **used Zylon®-containing body armor may not provide the intended level of ballistic resistance**. In addition, the results imply that a visual inspection of body armor and its ballistic panels does not indicate whether a particular piece of Zylon®-containing body armor has maintained its ballistic performance.

Part of the Body Armor Safety Initiative entailed an applied research component that examined material properties of Zylon® in order to understand the causes of the ballistic failures. Zylon® fibers show a systematic loss in tensile strength, tensile strain, and ballistic performance correlated with the breakage of specific bonds in the chemical structure of the material.

Preliminary findings from the applied research effort indicate that:

- It is likely that the ballistic performance degradation in Zylon®-containing armors is closely related to the chemical changes in poly-*p*-phenylene benzobisoxazole (PBO), the chemical basis of Zylon® fiber. The breakage of one particular part of the PBO molecule, known as the oxazole ring, correlates with degradation of the mechanical properties of Zylon® fibers. The breakage in the oxazole ring can be monitored using an analysis technique known as Fourier transform infrared (FTIR) spectroscopy.
- Preliminary investigations into Zylon® degradation mechanisms have suggested that oxazole-ring breakage occurs as a result of exposure to both moisture and light.
- When there was no potential for external moisture to contact Zylon® yarns, there was no significant change in the tensile strength of these yarns. External moisture may be necessary to facilitate the degradation of Zylon® fibers.

Based on the direction from the Attorney General and recommendations from the law enforcement community, NIJ has examined its body armor compliance testing program. The current NIJ testing program is based on the ballistic resistance of new armor and does not take into account performance degradation in used armor. NIJ is concerned that Zylon® and other materials may be incorporated into body armor, with minimal understanding of performance degradation that may result from environmental exposures. NIJ's research indicates that its testing program should take into account the possibility of ballistic performance degradation over time.

NIJ intends to adopt interim changes to its body armor compliance testing program, to aid in ensuring that officers are protected by body armor that maintains its ballistic performance during its entire warranty period. These actions are set forth in detail in Section VI of this report. Under the NIJ 2005 Interim Requirements for Bullet-Resistant Body Armor, armor models containing PBO (the chemical basis of Zylon®) will not be compliant, unless their manufacturers provide satisfactory evidence to NIJ that the models will maintain their ballistic performance over their declared warranty period.

U.S. Department of Justice
Office of Justice Programs
National Institute of Justice

Third Status Report to the Attorney General on
Body Armor Safety Initiative
Testing and Activities

All manufacturers will be required to submit information concerning materials used in the construction of any armor submitted for testing.

NIJ will recommend that those who purchase new bullet-resistant body armor select body armor models that comply with the NIJ 2005 Interim Requirements for Bullet-Resistant Body Armor. A list of models that comply with the requirements will be made available at http://www.justnet.org.

NIJ will also encourage manufacturers to adopt a quality-management system to ensure the consistent construction and performance of NIJ-compliant armor over its warranty period. In the future, NIJ will issue advisories to the field regarding materials used in the construction of body armor that appear to create a risk of death or serious injury as a result of degraded ballistic performance. Any body armor model that contains any material listed in such an advisory will be deemed no longer NIJ-compliant unless and until the manufacturer satisfies NIJ that the model will maintain its ballistic performance over its declared warranty period. NIJ will continue its research and evaluation program to determine what additional modifications to the requirements of NIJ's compliance testing program may be appropriate, to understand better the degradation mechanisms affecting existing or new ballistic materials, and to develop test methods for the ongoing performance of body armor.

NIJ continues to encourage public safety officers to wear their Zylon® - containing armor until it is replaced. Even armor that may have degraded ballistic performance is better than no armor.

I.   Introduction

In the summer of 2003, a Forest Hills, Pennsylvania, police officer was shot and seriously injured when a bullet penetrated the front panel of his Second Chance Ultima® armor, an armor made of multiple layers of fabric woven from Zylon® yarn. The incident was the first case reported to the National Institute of Justice (NIJ) in which NIJ-compliant body armor appears to have failed to prevent penetration from a bullet it was designed to defeat. Promptly after learning of this potential armor failure, NIJ initiated a review of the incident to determine the potential causes of failure.

On November 17, 2003, former Attorney General John Ashcroft announced the U.S. Department of Justice's Body Armor Safety Initiative in response to concerns from the law enforcement community regarding the effectiveness of their armor. He directed NIJ to initiate an examination of Zylon®-based bullet-resistant armor (both new and used), to analyze upgrade kits provided by manufacturers to retrofit Zylon®-based bullet-resistant armors, and to review the existing process by which bullet-resistant armor is certified to determine if the process needs modification. To accomplish these goals, NIJ has worked in collaboration with its technical partners, the Office of Law Enforcement Standards at the National Institute of Standards and Technology and the National Law Enforcement and Corrections Technology Center–National.

U.S. Department of Justice
Office of Justice Programs
National Institute of Justice

Third Status Report to the Attorney General on
Body Armor Safety Initiative
Testing and Activities

Previously, NIJ has issued two status reports to the Attorney General containing results from their body armor studies.[5] The reports, available at https://vests.ojp.gov/index.jsp, contained the following key findings:

- Ballistic-resistant material, including Zylon®, can degrade, thus reducing the ballistic resistance safety margin that manufacturers build into their armor designs. Certain analytical tools and techniques may be available to reveal and measure degradation in Zylon® and other ballistic-resistant fibers.

- The ultimate tensile strength of single yarns removed from the rear panel of the Forest Hills armor were up to 30-percent lower than yarns from "new" armors supplied by Second Chance Body Armor. Armors of the same type that failed in the Forest Hills incident were artificially aged and ballistically tested with the intent of focusing on five major variables that were believed to be potential contributors to the Forest Hills armor penetration. No penetrations were observed during testing. [Note: At the time, no definitive conclusions could be drawn, and efforts continue to explain the cause of the Forest Hills body armor penetration.]

- Upgrade kits did not appear to bring used Second Chance armor up to the level of performance of new Second Chance armor.

- In Phase I testing ("Worst Case Conditions"), 10 of the 18 used Zylon®-containing armors were penetrated by at least one round during the 6-shot ballistic testing series. The findings suggested that there may be degradation occurring in the ballistic-resistant performance of used Zylon®-containing body armor. Because of the small sample size, it was not possible to draw any statistically based conclusions about specific manufacturers, models, service life, or geographical regions.

Toyobo, the manufacturer of Zylon®, has reported that the strength of Zylon® decreases under conditions of high temperature, high humidity, and exposure to ultraviolet (UV) and visible light.[6] To combat the effects of light and humidity, ballistic panels made from Zylon® must be protected.

In addition, several body armor manufacturers have released statements, recalls, and warranty-adjustment notices as a result of Zylon®-related concerns. NIJ has reviewed this publicly available information but has not consulted with manufacturers concerning any specific actions taken by armor manufacturers concerning Zylon®-containing body armor.

---

[5] "Status Report to the Attorney General on Body Armor Safety Initiative Testing and Activities," March 11, 2004, and "Supplement I: Status Report to the Attorney General on Body Armor Safety Initiative Testing and Activities," December 27, 2004.

[6] Technical Information Bulletin, "PBO Fiber Zylon®," Toyobo Co., Ltd., revised 2001.

U.S. Department of Justice
Office of Justice Programs
National Institute of Justice

Third Status Report to the Attorney General on
Body Armor Safety Initiative
Testing and Activities

NIJ has found that over 260 different models of Zylon®-containing ballistic body armor from 16 different manufacturers comply with NIJ's current standard, NIJ Standard–0101.04, or its predecessor, NIJ Standard–0101.03. Preliminary information from the U.S. Department of Justice's Bulletproof Vest Partnership Program indicates that, as of 2003, more than 240,000 Zylon®-containing armors may have been in field use, and information from additional sources suggests the number may have been greater.

This supplement will report on findings from NIJ's broad-based ballistic testing of Zylon®-containing armors obtained from law enforcement agencies across the United States. In addition, this supplement will describe critical findings concerning performance degradation mechanisms of Zylon®-containing armors based on NIJ's applied research.

II. Supplemental Results From Phase I Testing

Since the first two status reports were submitted to the Attorney General, NIJ has tested 10 additional Zylon®-containing armors as part of Phase I of its multiphase test plan. Testing of the 10 armors concludes Phase I of NIJ's Body Armor Safety Initiative.

All of the Zylon®-containing armors tested in Phase I showed a general decline in performance. The front panels from 28 armors (18 originally reported plus the 10 additional armors) were tested with the 6-shot ballistic testing protocol described in the first report to the Attorney General. Penetrations were observed in 12 of the 28 samples (43%). Results are shown in Figure 1 and Appendix A. Backface signature results are presented for armors that passed penetration testing.

U.S. Department of Justice
Office of Justice Programs
National Institute of Justice

Third Status Report to the Attorney General on
Body Armor Safety Initiative
Testing and Activities

Figure 1. Summary of Phase I (Worst Case) P-BFS Testing

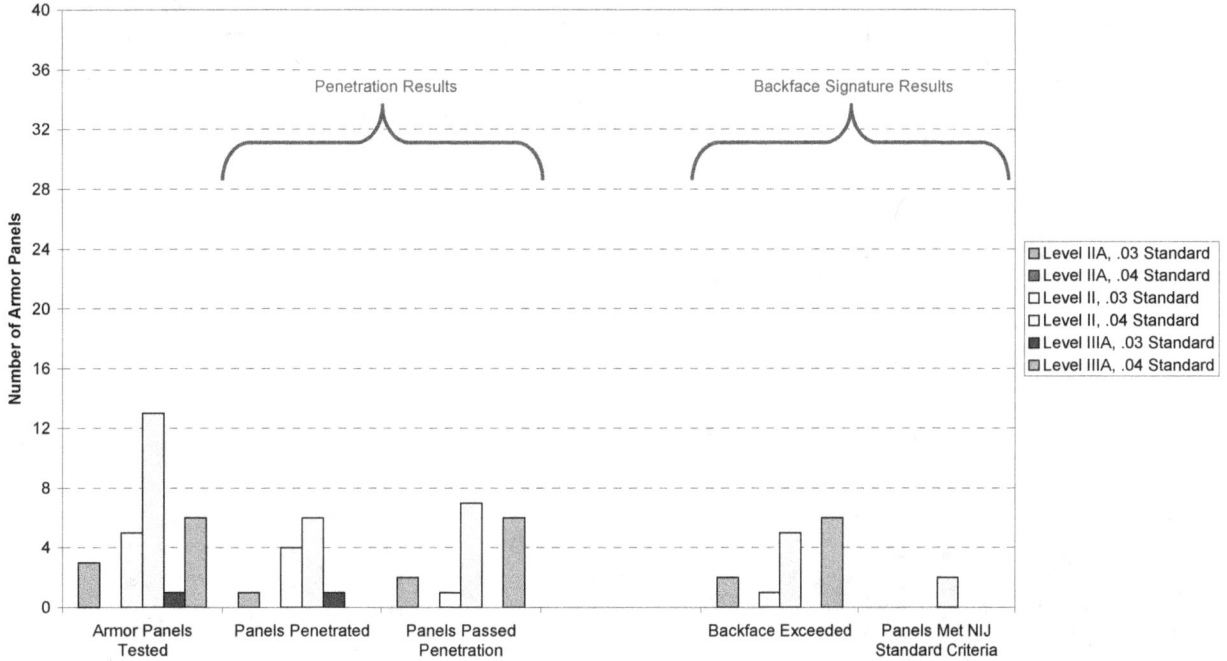

NIJ measured the tensile strength of the yarns from 22 of the 28 front armor panels tested in the 6-shot penetration test series. The mean ultimate tensile strength and comparison to a baseline value is shown in Figure 2 and Appendix B. There is no way to know the actual "new armor" yarn tensile strength for each armor panel, so a baseline value of 4.78 GPa[7] was assumed to apply to all woven Zylon® samples. This baseline value was determined on the basis of average tensile strength measurements of yarns that were taken from woven Zylon® fabric. The fabrics were cut from newly constructed Zylon® armor panels that had been manufactured in September 2003 and tensile tested in October 2003. The baseline tensile strength provides some indication of how much tensile strength is lost after the armor has been manufactured. For yarns from the 22 panels studied, ultimate tensile strength losses averaged 41% (with a minimum loss of 11% and a maximum loss of 61%). Reductions in mechanical properties, such as tensile strength, may have a detrimental effect on ballistic performance.

The back panels from the 28 armor samples were subjected to ballistic limit testing.[8] Figure 3 compares these ballistic limit values to baseline ballistic limit values from new armors of the same type (available for 19 of the 28 armor samples tested). The diagonal line in the figure

---

[7] GPa, or gigapascal, is a unit that describes the force exerted over an area.

[8] Ballistic limit testing estimates the velocity at which a given bullet is expected to completely penetrate a body armor panel 50 percent of the time. These tests used a conventional full metal jacketed 9-mm bullet weighing approximately 8 grams (124 grains).

U.S. Department of Justice
Office of Justice Programs
National Institute of Justice

Third Status Report to the Attorney General on
Body Armor Safety Initiative
Testing and Activities

represents the baseline ballistic limit, i.e., the ballistic limit that would be seen if the armor had performed as well as it did when new. Therefore, points above the diagonal line represent improved performance, while points below the line represent degraded performance. Because of the limitations of the ballistic limit test methodology, differences of approximately 100 ft/s are probably not significant, but greater differences suggest a significant loss in performance. Nine of the 19 armors exhibit such a performance loss. Those nine are shown as a shaded red circle in Figure 3.

Figure 2. **Tensile Strength of Zylon® Yarns**

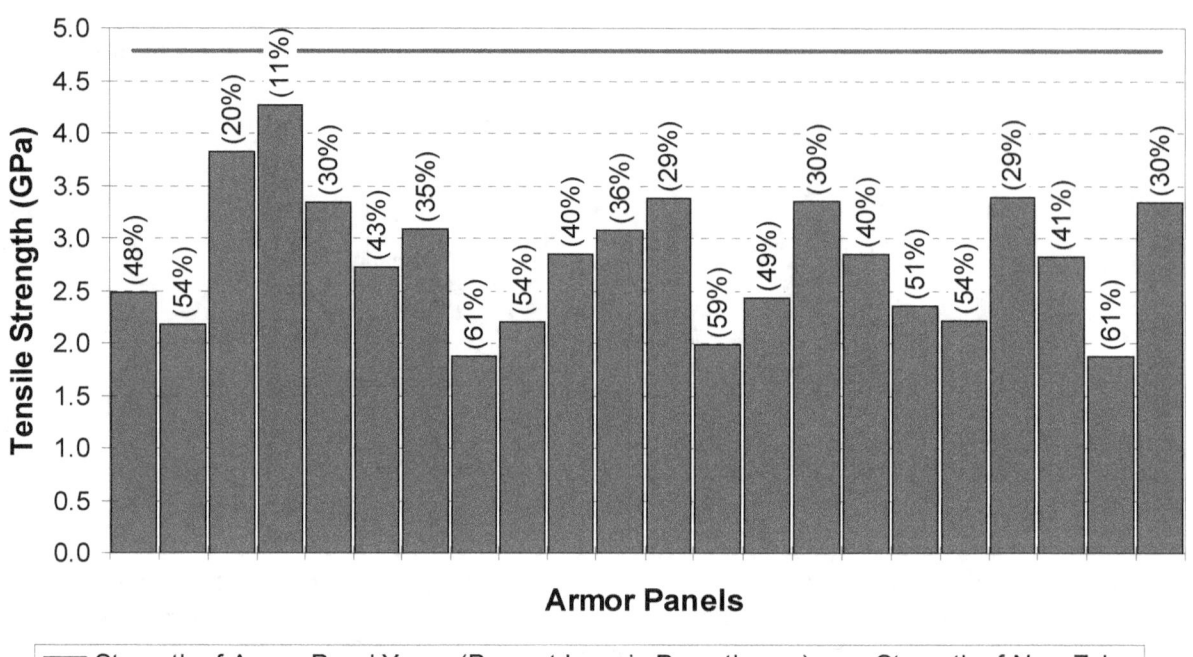

U.S. Department of Justice
Office of Justice Programs
National Institute of Justice

Third Status Report to the Attorney General on
Body Armor Safety Initiative
Testing and Activities

Figure 3. Comparison of Baseline and Field Return Ballistic Limit (V50) Values

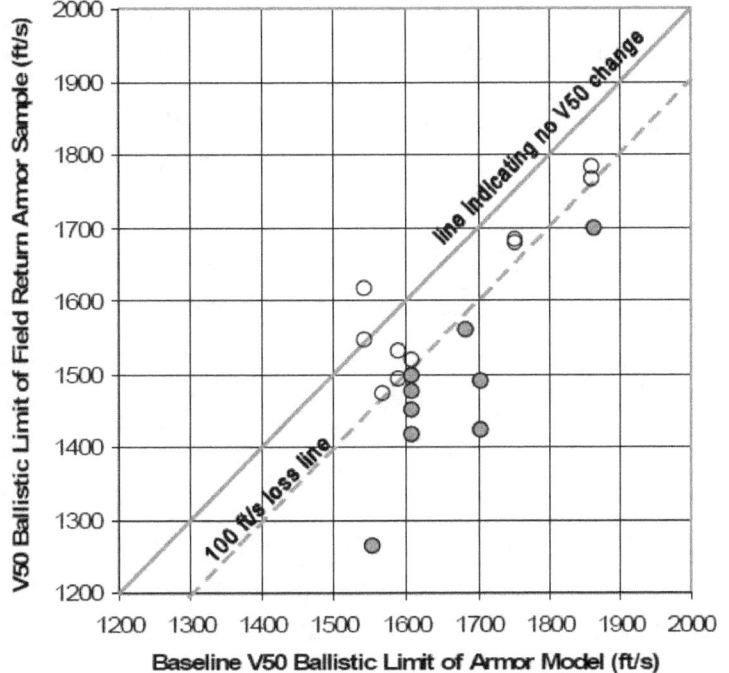

Conclusions based on Phase I results are limited by several concerns with the test methodology: sample sizes were limited, they were not random, they did not represent the wide variety of models and manufacturers, and the environments to which these armor specimens were exposed are not known. Despite the limitations, these results continue to support the working theory that degradation is occurring in the ballistic performance of used Zylon®-containing armors.

III.   Phase II Testing Results

Following the test failures observed in Phase I, NIJ's Phase II test plan was designed to examine the effects of age, climate, and armor design on armor performance. This broad-based testing phase was intended to determine the ongoing performance and reliability of Zylon® body armor in field use based on a statistically representative sample of armors in use by law enforcement. However, this phase was hindered by the lack of available armor to test. The test plan initially called for the evaluation of nearly 500 armor samples, but NIJ was able to obtain less than 80 armors for two primary reasons: first, some major manufacturers of Zylon® armors initiated buyout or replacement programs for many of their Zylon®-containing armor models, which greatly reduced the number of available armors in the field. Second, NIJ found discrepancies

U.S. Department of Justice
Office of Justice Programs
National Institute of Justice

Third Status Report to the Attorney General on
Body Armor Safety Initiative
Testing and Activities

between what armor models were believed to be in use and what law enforcement agencies actually had in service.

A total of 75 Zylon®-containing body armors were examined during the initial part of Phase II testing. One panel was randomly selected from each armor and subjected to penetration-backface signature[9] (P-BFS) testing in a protocol similar to that used during Phase I testing. Each panel was tested using the two different calibers associated with the armor's classification (Type IIA, Type II, or Type IIIA). Three shots of each caliber consistent with the NIJ Standard were fired (for a total of six shots), with one of the three shots for each caliber fired at a 30-degree impact angle. Unlike Phase I, during the Phase II P-BFS tests, all of the armor panels were tested in a wet condition in accordance with the NIJ standard.

During the final part of Phase II testing, the companion panels will be subjected to ballistic limit testing to determine if, and how much, the ballistic limit has shifted since the armor model was originally tested for compliance to an NIJ standard. Zylon® yarns will be taken from selected armor panels and subjected to tensile testing. These results will be described in a subsequent report.

A large number of the tested armor samples experienced penetrations and/or backface signatures that exceeded the maximum allowable limit of 44 mm (1.73 in) specified in the NIJ standard. Penetrations were observed in 48 of the 75 (64%) armor panels; 34 (45%) were penetrated more than once. Ten of the 75 (13%) armor panels were penetrated by all six rounds. Of the 27 armor panels that were not penetrated, all but two experienced at least one excessive backface signature. Figure 4 shows the number of armors tested from each threat level and test standard and summarizes the results of the P-BFS tests. Appendix C contains the complete results. Appendix D summarizes the data for specific armor types.

While these results do not conclusively prove that all Zylon®-containing body armor models have performance issues, they clearly show that ***used Zylon®-containing body armor may not provide the intended level of ballistic resistance***.

---

[9] Backface Signature (BFS): when armor is tested, it is mounted on clay backing materials whose consistency is controlled. After the shot, the depth of the clay deformation behind the armor panel is measured and recorded as the BFS.

U.S. Department of Justice
Office of Justice Programs
National Institute of Justice

Third Status Report to the Attorney General on
Body Armor Safety Initiative
Testing and Activities

Figure 4. Summary of Phase II P-BFS Testing

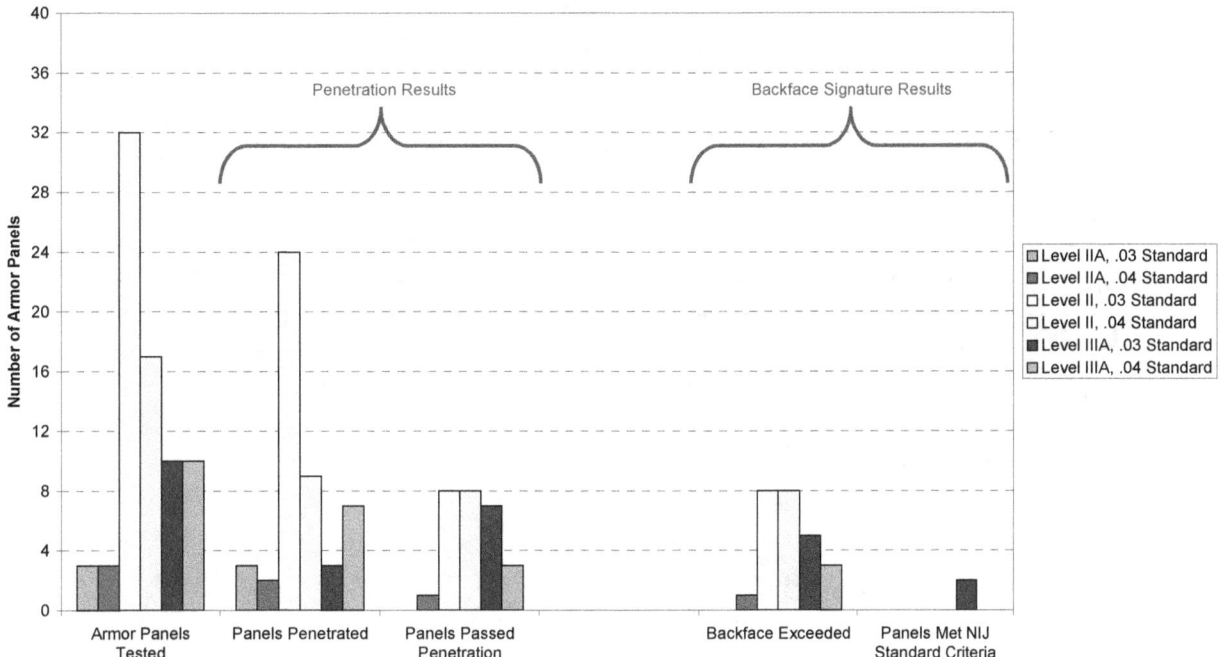

A. Analysis of Results by Age of Armor

The 75 armors tested in the Phase II P-BFS tests ranged in age from 17 to 71 months. Fifty-three were less than 5 years old, or within the standard warranty period for most body armor (although the warranty period for some of these vests is as low as 30 months). Of these 53 armors, 35 (66%) were penetrated. Twelve armors were between 60 and 70 months old, exceeding the warranty period by up to 10 months. Of these 12 older armors, eight (67%) were penetrated. The age of 10 armors could not be determined; five of the 10 (50%) were penetrated.

Table 1 lists the performance of the tested armors by age. There is no clear correlation between armor age and penetration rate. These results imply that used Zylon®-containing armor may not provide the intended level of ballistic protection, regardless of age, although the number of armors in this data set with less than two years of service life is quite limited.

U.S. Department of Justice
Office of Justice Programs
National Institute of Justice

Third Status Report to the Attorney General on
Body Armor Safety Initiative
Testing and Activities

Table 1. Results of Penetration Testing with Respect to Age

Age of armors (months)	Number tested	Number passed Penetration	Number Penetrated	Percent Penetrated
less than 24	2	1	1	50%
24 to 30	4	1	3	75%
30 to 36	6	3	3	50%
36 to 42	5	1	4	80%
42 to 48	15	4	11	73%
48 to 54	8	1	7	88%
54 to 60	13	7	6	46%
60 to 66	8	1	7	88%
66 to 72	4	3	1	25%
unknown	10	5	5	50%

Note: Shaded areas are armors whose age is beyond the standard warranty period of 60 months

B. Analysis of Results by Percentage of Zylon® in Armor

The percentage of Zylon® material in the ballistic resistant panels varied greatly between the armor models. For the purposes of this study, the percentage of Zylon® material in a model of armor was calculated by dividing the number of layers in the ballistic panel that were constructed from either woven Zylon® yarns or laminated sheets of Zylon® fibers by the total number of material layers. Four of the armors tested contained less than 15% Zylon®. Of these, none experienced penetrations during testing. No armors were tested that contained between 15% and 25% Zylon®. Three of nine armors containing 25% to 30% Zylon® layers experienced penetrations. For the groups of armors containing more than 30% Zylon®, the penetration rates ranged from 60% to 100%. Table 2 lists the penetration rates for groups of armors with various percentages of Zylon® layers. These results clearly indicate that used armors containing more than a small percentage of Zylon® material are unlikely to reliably provide the intended level of ballistic protection.

U.S. Department of Justice
Office of Justice Programs
National Institute of Justice

Third Status Report to the Attorney General on
Body Armor Safety Initiative
Testing and Activities

Table 2. Results of Penetration Testing with Respect to Quantity of Zylon®

Fraction of Layers Containing Zylon®	Number Tested	Number Passed Penetration	Number Penetrated	Percent Penetrated
Less than 15%	4	4	0	0
15% to 25%	0	-	-	-
25% to 30%	9	6	3	33%
30% to 35%	11	0	11	100%
35% to 50%	5	2	3	60%
50% to 75%	11	3	8	73%
75% to 99%	4	0	4	100%
100%	31	12	19	61%

C. Analysis of Results by Threat Round

During NIJ compliance testing of levels IIA, II, and IIIA armor, each armor model is shot with two threats: a 9 mm bullet and either a 40 S&W, 357 Magnum, or 44 Magnum bullet (hereafter referred to as the "other" round) depending on the armor's threat level. These threat rounds are intended to subject the armor to both penetrative and blunt trauma threats.

Table 3 lists which threat round penetrated armors for each of the threat levels. Of the 48 armors that were penetrated, 25 were penetrated by both rounds, six by the 9 mm round only, and 17 by the other round only. These results indicate that both threat rounds may be nearly as penetrative. Therefore, both rounds should be considered to determine the ballistic performance of a particular armor.

Table 3. Results of Penetration Testing with Respect to Threat Round

Armor Type		Number Tested	Number Passed Penetration	Number of Armors Penetrated			
Threat Level	NIJ Standard			Either Round	9 mm	Other Threat	Both Rounds
All Armors		75	27 (36 %)	48 (64 %)	31 (41 %)	42 (56 %)	25 (33 %)
IIA	.03	3	0 (0 %)	3 (100 %)	3 (100 %)	1 (33 %)	1 (33 %)
	.04	3	1 (33 %)	2 (67 %)	2 (67 %)	0 (0 %)	0 (0 %)
II	.03	32	8 (25 %)	24 (75 %)	13 (41 %)	23 (72 %)	12 (38 %)
	.04	17	8 (47 %)	9 (53 %)	4 (24 %)	9 (53 %)	4 (24 %)
IIIA	.03	10	7 (70 %)	3 (30 %)	3 (30 %)	3 (30 %)	3 (30 %)
	.04	10	3 (30 %)	7 (70 %)	6 (60 %)	6 (60 %)	5 (50 %)

U.S. Department of Justice
Office of Justice Programs
National Institute of Justice

Third Status Report to the Attorney General on
Body Armor Safety Initiative
Testing and Activities

D. Analysis of Results by Armor Condition

All armors tested as part of the DOJ Body Armor Safety Initiative were visually inspected and given a condition rating that indicated how well worn or damaged the armor was before testing. The condition ratings range from Condition 1 for armor that appeared to be "like new" to Condition 4 for armors that showed signs of extreme wear or abuse. The armors tested during Phase II P-BFS tests ranged from Condition 2 (light to moderate wear) to Condition 4; the vast majority rated Condition 3 (significant wear - daily use for extended period) or Condition 4.

Table 4 lists the test results based on the armor condition rating. More than half the armor in each condition category was penetrated. There appears to be no correlation between condition ratings and performance. The results imply that a visual inspection of the armor and its ballistic panels cannot determine if a particular piece of Zylon®-containing body armor will perform acceptably.

Table 4. Results of Penetration Testing with Respect to Armor Condition

Condition Rating	Explanation	Number Tested	Number Passed Penetration	Number Penetrated	Percent Penetrated
Note that the armor condition rating is based on a visual inspection.					
1	Armors that show no visible signs of wear and is in new or "like new" condition.	0	0	0	-
2	Armors that show light to moderate signs of wear.	10	4	6	60%
3	Armors that show significant signs of wear (daily use for extended period).	34	15	19	56%
4	Armors that show signs of extreme wear or abuse.	31	8	23	74%

IV.   Results of Phase I and Phase II Ballistic Testing

Although the test methodologies and sampling criteria were slightly different between Phase I and Phase II, combined ballistic test results for the 103 Zylon®-containing armor samples demonstrate that much of the used Zylon®-containing armor did not maintain ballistic performance in field use. Table 5 and Figure 5 show the combined test results from Phases I and II. Key findings are:

- Zylon®-containing armor may not provide the intended level of ballistic protection.

U.S. Department of Justice
Office of Justice Programs
National Institute of Justice

Third Status Report to the Attorney General on
Body Armor Safety Initiative
Testing and Activities

- Ballistic limits of used armor samples were generally less than the original compliance samples. In many cases there were declines in ballistic limit values of 100 ft/s or more.

- Zylon® yarns taken from used armor samples exhibited degraded tensile strength characteristics.

- Age and visual examination did not correlate with demonstrated ballistic performance, thus they appear to be ineffective indicators of potential ballistic performance.

- Of the used armor samples that were not penetrated, nearly all exhibited higher backface signatures than permitted by the NIJ Compliance Testing Program.

Table 5. Overview of Phase I and Phase II P-BFS Tests

	Phase I	Phase II	Combined
Armor Selection	Worst case armors from selected agencies	Much larger number of Zylon® armors in BVP database	
Test Conditions	Front panel tested dry	Random panel tested wet	
Armors Tested	28	75	103
Armors Penetrated	**12 (43%)**	**48 (64%)**	**60 (58%)**
Passed Penetration	16 (57%)	27 (36%)	43 (42%)
Armors with Excessive BFS	14 (50%)	25 (33%)	39 (38%)
Armors Met All NIJ Criteria	2 (7%)	2 (3%)	4 (4%)

U.S. Department of Justice
Office of Justice Programs
National Institute of Justice

Third Status Report to the Attorney General on
Body Armor Safety Initiative
Testing and Activities

Figure 5. Summary of Phase I and II Combined P-BFS Testing

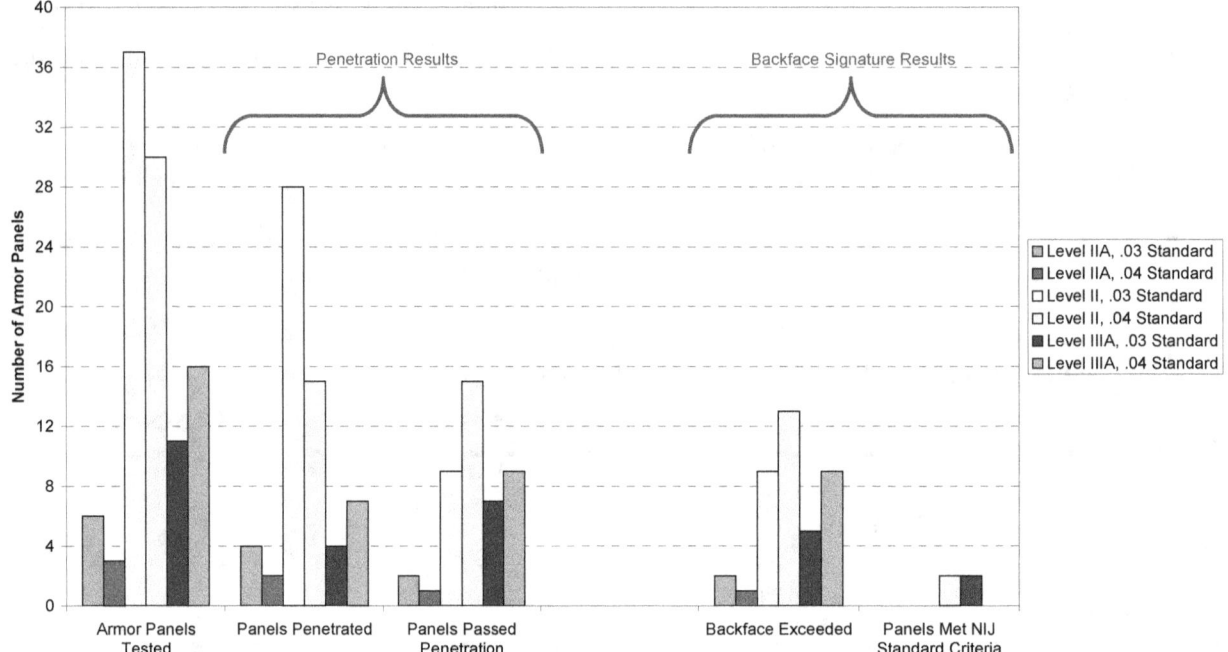

V.   Applied Research

While NIJ's examination and testing of used Zylon®-containing body armor does show that there is degradation in performance, it is critical to understand the fundamental nature of Zylon® degradation and how the degradation relates to ballistic performance. To complement the ballistic test program, NIJ initiated a number of applied research activities to:

- Identify analytical techniques for characterizing the chemical, physical, and mechanical properties of PBO and other ballistic materials.

- Determine what factors may contribute to the degradation Zylon® (e.g. heat, humidity, UV and visible light, mechanical stress).

- Correlate changes in chemical and mechanical fiber properties to the performance of ballistic resistant materials.

- Determine if the presence of moisture or other trace materials in the virgin fiber may contribute to performance degradation, even without external influences.

- Determine if an accelerated aging process or other nondestructive processes can be developed to predict and evaluate the ongoing ballistic performance of used body armor.

U.S. Department of Justice
Office of Justice Programs
National Institute of Justice

Third Status Report to the Attorney General on
Body Armor Safety Initiative
Testing and Activities

The results of the research are documented in a report[10] and a technical paper,[11] both of which will be published shortly. Most of the research described here is ongoing and will be updated as new findings become available. While NIJ's initial research has focused primarily on Zylon®, future phases of this applied research program will examine other ballistic-resistant materials.

The ballistic material called by the trade name Zylon® is also known by its chemical name, poly(p-phenylene benzobisoxazole), or PBO. PBO is a polymer that can be thought of as a long chain of repeat units that are bonded together in a linear arrangement. One repeat unit is depicted in Figure 6. Millions of these polymer chains arrange themselves into a long thin fiber. In some cases the individual fibers are incorporated into nonwoven ballistic resistant fabrics, such as the case with Z Shield®.[12] In other cases, hundreds of these fibers are bundled together to form a yarn, which is then woven into fabric, as is the case with the traditional woven Zylon® fabric.

The chemical structure of PBO provides high thermal stability and outstanding mechanical properties. PBO fibers are extremely strong, tough, and stiff, with certain mechanical properties, such as tensile strength and elastic modulus,[13] that are superior to those of para-aramid fibers (e.g., Kevlar®, Twaron®) or ultra-high molecular weight polyethylene fibers (e.g. Dyneema®, Spectra®).

Figure 6. Chemical structure of poly(p-phenylene benzobisoxazole), or PBO, repeat unit

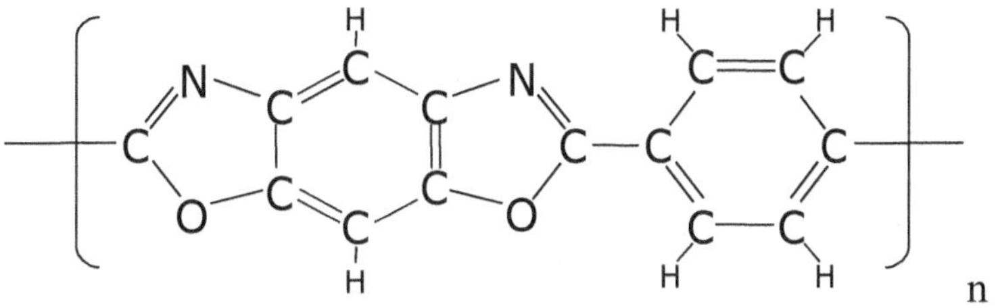

A number of questions exist concerning the hydrolytic and ultraviolet (UV)-visible light stability of PBO, or described differently, the susceptibility of PBO to degrade when exposed to moisture and light. Toyobo has reported tensile strength degradation of PBO fiber following exposure to

---

[10] Chin, J., et al., "Chemical Analysis of Poly(p-phenylene benzobisoxazole) Fibers Used in Ballistic Applications," NISTIR TBD (forthcoming).

[11] Holmes, G.A., et al., "Ballistic Fibers: A Review of the Thermal, Ultraviolet and Hydrolytic Stability of the Benzoxazole Ring Structure," accepted for publication in the *Journal of Materials Science* (forthcoming).

[12] Z Shield is a registered trademark of Honeywell International Inc.

[13] Modulus is a technical term that describes the stiffness of a material.

U.S. Department of Justice
Office of Justice Programs
National Institute of Justice

Third Status Report to the Attorney General on
Body Armor Safety Initiative
Testing and Activities

heat and moisture[14]. Only a few studies in the peer-reviewed literature provide any data on the hydrolytic stability of PBO in aqueous and acidic conditions.[15] As far back as 1995, researchers at NASA evaluated the chemical resistance of PBO and observed significant losses in tensile strength following immersion in water, hydrochloric acid, nitric acid, sulfuric acid, sodium chloride and sodium hypochlorite.[16]

In general, PBO and similar materials undergo hydrolysis[17] in conditions ranging from neutral to acidic and at ambient as well as elevated temperatures. One study documents the effects of ultraviolet and visible light on PBO fibers, where substantial (> 90 %) loss in tensile strength was observed following harsh UV exposure conditions.[16]

A. Relationship Between Ballistic Capability and Mechanical Properties

This report discusses mechanical properties of fibers, since materials used in textile-based armor systems have certain desirable mechanical properties that relate to ballistic performance. The relationship between mechanical properties and ballistic performance has been established by both experiment and theory. For example, Cunniff empirically demonstrated this relationship by developing a parameter known as U^* that correlates with the ballistic performance[18] of many armor systems.[19] Phoenix and Porwal established a theoretical basis for U^* from first principles modeling of an armor's response to ballistic impact.[20] In addition, a number of experiments have demonstrated good agreement with the ballistic performance predicted using the U^* parameter. The expression for U^* is as follows:

$$U^* = \frac{\sigma_{uts}\varepsilon_f}{2\rho}\sqrt{\frac{E}{\rho}}$$

---

[14] http://www.toyobo.co.jp/e/seihin/kc/pbo/pdf/Attachment_1970KB.pdf

[15] Y.-H. So, S.J. Martin, K. Owen, P.B. Smith, and C.L. Karas, J. "A study of benzobisoxazole and benzobisthiazole compounds and polymers under hydrolytic conditions." *Journal of Polymer Science Part A: Polymer Chemistry*, 37, 2637-2643 (1999).

[16] E. Orndoff, *NASA Technical Memorandum 104814*, (September 1995).

[17] Hydrolysis is the decomposition of a chemical compound by reaction with water.

[18] Specifically, the ballistic performance here refers to the V50 ballistic limit of the armor system against fragment-simulating projectiles.

[19] Cunniff, P.M. and M.A. Auerbach, "23rd Army Science Conference," Assistant Secretary of the Army (Acquisition, Logistics, and Technology), Orlando, FL, (December 2002).

[20] Phoenix, S.L. and P.K. Porwal, "A New Membrane Model for the Ballistic Impact Response and V50 Performance of Multi-Ply Fibrous Systems." *International Journal of Solids and Structures*, 40, 6723 (2003).

U.S. Department of Justice
Office of Justice Programs
National Institute of Justice

Third Status Report to the Attorney General on
Body Armor Safety Initiative
Testing and Activities

In this equation, σ_{uts} is the fiber's ultimate tensile strength; , ε is the fiber's ultimate tensile strain, a measure of the amount a fiber stretches before breaking; E is the modulus, a measure of how much a fiber stretches under a load; and ρ is the density of the fiber. Thus, changes in any of these physical properties will change the ballistic performance of a material. The U^* parameter relates changes in certain physical properties of a fiber to the ballistic performance of an armor made from that fiber. Therefore, Cunniff's equation provides a basis for evaluating Zylon® or any other fiber used in body armor.

B. Comparative Analysis of Zylon® from Different Sources

A comparative analysis of PBO materials was performed as part of the applied research effort. The studies used yarn samples from the following sources:

- **Officer's armor:** The back panel of the Forest Hills officer's armor that was penetrated. The armor was manufactured in November 2002. The front panel, where the bullet penetration occurred, is currently being retained as evidence and could not be obtained for analysis at the time of this writing.

- **New armor:** A new, unworn armor of the same model and construction as the officer's armor, style SMU-IIA+105130, manufactured in September 2003.

- **Archive armor:** An armor from the National Law Enforcement and Corrections Technology Center (NLECTC) Compliance Test Program archives, style SMU-IIA+105130, manufactured in March 2001, and submitted for compliance testing in May 2001.

- **Virgin yarn:** PBO spool yarn, manufactured in August 2003 and provided to the National Institute of Standards and Technology (NIST) by the fiber manufacturer in May 2004 for this study.

C. Changes in Mechanical Properties of Zylon® Yarn

The mechanical properties of the yarns were measured and compared to virgin yarn. The results are shown in Table 6. The yarns from the officer's armor are clearly lower in tensile strength and tensile strain than the yarns from the new and archive armors, as well as the virgin yarn. The tensile strength of the yarns from the archive armor is also lower than that of the new armor and virgin yarns. When yarn is woven into fabric, there may be as much as 10–20 % loss in tensile strength due to mechanical fiber damage. The difference between the tensile properties of the virgin yarn and the new armor yarn, approximately 10%, may be due to this mechanical damage; however, this type of mechanical damage alone would not explain the further reduction in tensile strength of yarns from the archive vest and the officer's vest.

U.S. Department of Justice
Office of Justice Programs
National Institute of Justice

Third Status Report to the Attorney General on
Body Armor Safety Initiative
Testing and Activities

Interestingly, the moduli—or stiffness—of the yarns from the three vests are not substantially different. Toyobo previously reported results of environmental conditioning tests on Zylon® fiber.[21] In that report, they stated that the "tensile modulus for Zylon® fiber remains constant" and that "energy dissipation remains constant and extremely high." The results in Table 6 support the first statement, but not the second. The moduli are relatively constant, indicating that the stiffness of the Zylon® yarns from the different vests is about the same, but the energy dissipating characteristics of the yarns are dramatically different, as indicated by the "Energy to Break Point" column in Table 6. Essentially, this quantity is the area under the stress versus strain curve. When the tensile strength and strain at break are each reduced, the energy-absorbing ability of the yarn will also be reduced. In this case, yarns from the officer's vest can absorb only about half of the energy before breaking compared to yarns from the new vest.

Table 6: Tensile Properties of Armor Yarns[22]

Source of Fiber	Tensile Strength (GPa)	Strain at Break (%)	Modulus at Break (GPa)	Energy to Break Point (N m)
Officer	3.22	2.50	136.61	0.31
New	4.78	3.29	141.80	0.61
Archive	3.65	2.65	141.60	0.37
Virgin	5.34	3.52	147.11	0.91

D.   Chemical Changes in Zylon® When Examined with Infrared Spectroscopy

A large body of scientific literature reveals that the oxazole ring, the five-member ring that appears within the chemical structure of PBO, has characteristics that cause it to be susceptible to degradation due to moisture and light exposure. Determining if there is scientific evidence of this degradation in real armor samples is important. Fourier transform infrared (FTIR) spectroscopy is a common technique used in crime laboratories. FTIR relies on the fact that different types of chemical bonds preferentially absorb infrared light of different wavelengths, and by measuring which wavelengths are absorbed, a characteristic "spectrum," or fingerprint,

---

[21] Toyobo Co., Ltd., Letter to Customers, March 9, 2004,
http://www.toyobo.co.jp/e/seihin/kc/pbo/pdf/Letter_on_modulus_030904.pdf and
http://www.toyobo.co.jp/e/seihin/kc/pbo/pdf/modulus_graph.pdf

[22] Values presented are mean values. Chin, J., et al., "Chemical Analysis of Poly(*p*-phenylene benzobisoxazole) Fibers Used in Ballistic Applications," NISTIR TBD (forthcoming).

U.S. Department of Justice
Office of Justice Programs
National Institute of Justice

Third Status Report to the Attorney General on
Body Armor Safety Initiative
Testing and Activities

for the material being studied can be obtained. By comparing the spectrum to other spectra of known model compounds,[23] the identity of the subject material can be determined.

FTIR has been applied successfully to the effort to measure changes in the oxazole ring and to look for evidence that helps identify the degradation mechanisms. PBO produces an FTIR spectrum similar to that shown in Figure 7. The oxazole ring is circled. Key spectral components are highlighted that correspond to certain bonds on the oxazole ring.

Figure 7: Typical IR spectra of PBO

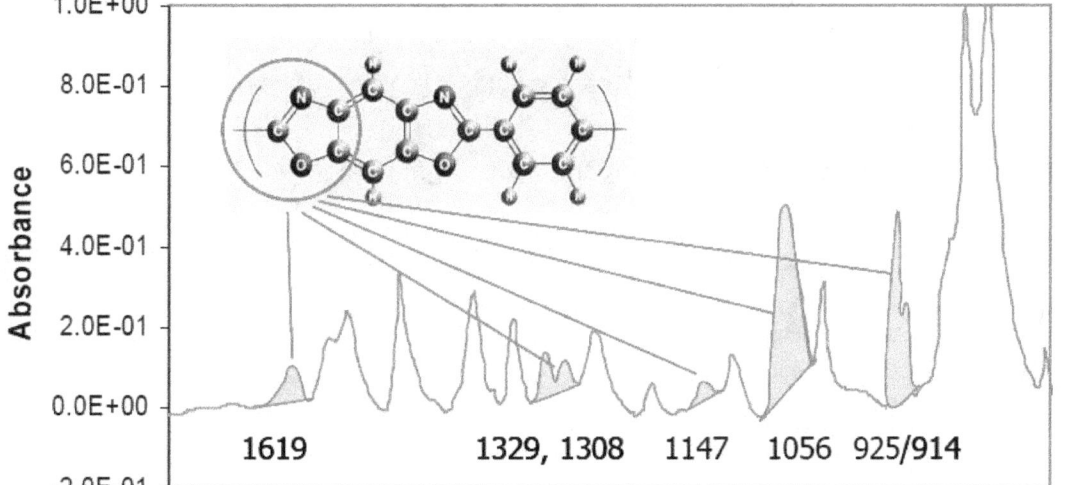

Chemical changes due to polymer degradation are often difficult to detect from a simple visual inspection of the FTIR spectra because the differences in the various peaks and valleys are minor in many cases. Even subtle differences can be indicative of significant chemical changes. Figure 8 demonstrates this: the FTIR spectra from all four yarn samples appear to be the same (the lines are offset from each other vertically to better show their shapes). To solve this problem, the spectrum of each material is subtracted from the spectrum of a control sample. This approach highlights even minor differences between spectra. This technique was validated during the artificial aging process described in Supplement I in which FTIR was used to monitor the progressive breaking of the oxazole ring in PBO over time.

---

[23] Model compounds are stand-alone compounds that can be an effective method for studying unique characteristics of another compound and for studying small changes that may occur in a complex polymer.

U.S. Department of Justice
Office of Justice Programs
National Institute of Justice

Third Status Report to the Attorney General on
Body Armor Safety Initiative
Testing and Activities

Figure 9 shows the spectra that result when the FTIR spectrum of the virgin yarn is subtracted from each of the armor yarn spectra. A flat spectral difference line at "0" absorbance would indicate that there are no differences between the virgin yarn control sample and the other sample. Downward-pointing peaks in the spectra indicate chemical bonds that have been lost while upward-pointing peaks are indicative of bonds that have increased. Figure 9 indicates that there is a progressive change. The new vest yarn is most similar to the virgin yarn, the archive vest yarn is next, and the officer's vest yarn is the most changed.

In this study, the FTIR data show that the oxazole ring degraded in the officer's armor yarn compared to unused armor. Thus, it is likely that the ballistic performance degradation in PBO armors is closely related to the chemical changes in the PBO fiber resulting from oxazole ring breakage. This change can be monitored using FTIR, implying that this analysis technique may provide a basis for nondestructive monitoring of ballistic performance.

Figure 8. FTIR spectra of armor yarns, compared with virgin yarn

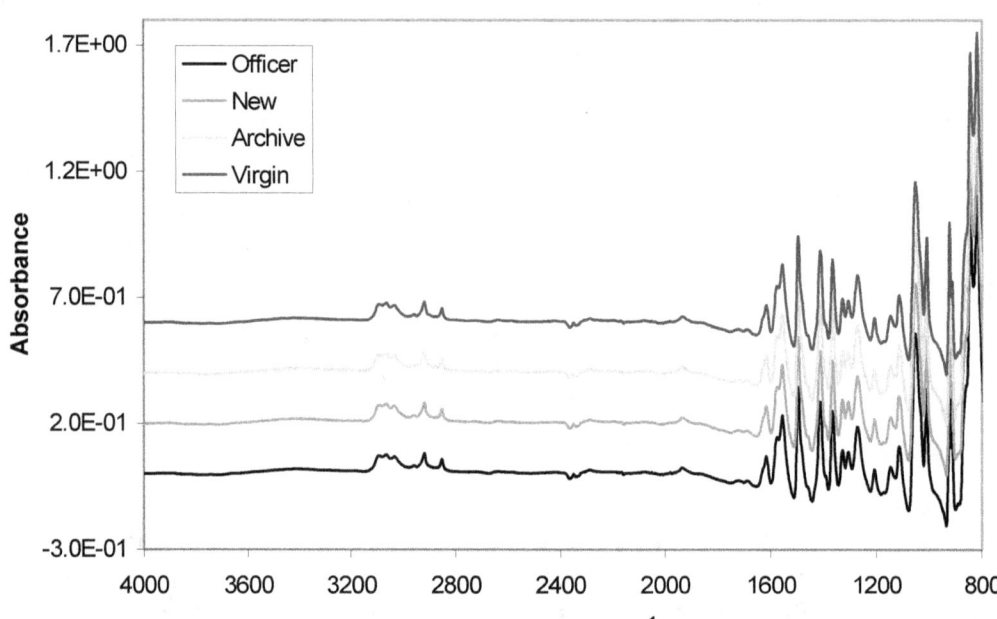

U.S. Department of Justice
Office of Justice Programs
National Institute of Justice

Third Status Report to the Attorney General on
Body Armor Safety Initiative
Testing and Activities

Figure 9. Difference spectra of armor yarns

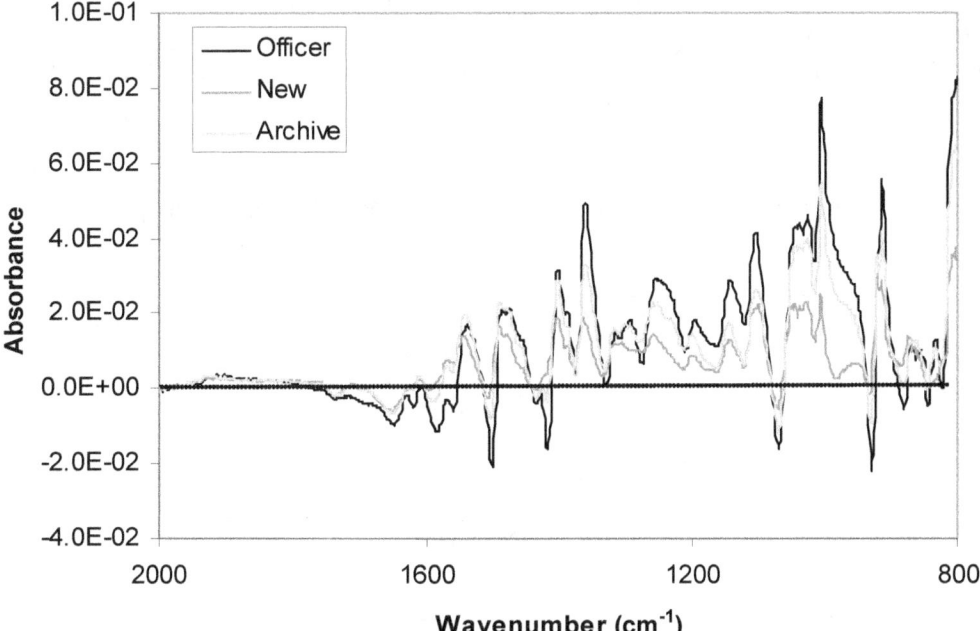

E. Moisture Effect on Armor Degradation

In the Forest Hills study reported previously, new armor was artificially aged in a temperature-humidity chamber. The artificial aging process provided experimental evidence that moisture could drive the degradation of Zylon®-containing body armor. Mechanical properties were monitored to confirm that the new armor panels had been weakened to match the weakened state of the officer's body armor from the Forest Hills incident. Once that weakened state had been achieved, the temperature-humidity chamber was adjusted in an attempt to halt the hydrolysis process. Some of the armor panels that were not used for the Forest Hills ballistics tests remained in the temperature-humidity chamber for an extended period of time. After 157 days, the humidity level was changed to a very low value (5% relative humidity). As seen in Figure 10, the Zylon® yarn tensile strength did not change in low-humidity conditions.

Based on this finding, the following questions were posed: 1) If the Zylon® fiber were prevented from coming into contact with external moisture, would degradation be slowed down or prevented? 2) Is there enough moisture trapped in the Zylon® fiber to promote degradation, even if there were no exposure to external moisture?

To study these questions, virgin Zylon® yarns were placed inside glass tubes, backfilled with argon, and then sealed so that there was no potential for external moisture to contact the yarn. The only moisture present would be moisture that was initially present in the fiber structure or on

U.S. Department of Justice
Office of Justice Programs
National Institute of Justice

Third Status Report to the Attorney General on
Body Armor Safety Initiative
Testing and Activities

the fiber surface. This would represent the "ideal" if one could effect a perfect hermetic seal for PBO in body armor. The sealed tubes were held at a constant temperature of 55°C and periodically sampled. Over a period of seven months there was no significant change in the tensile strength of these yarns, as indicated by the flat line for the "Sealed Tube" study in Figure 10.

Figure 10: Tensile Strength Retained by Zylon® Yarns (humidity-exposed vs. sealed tube)

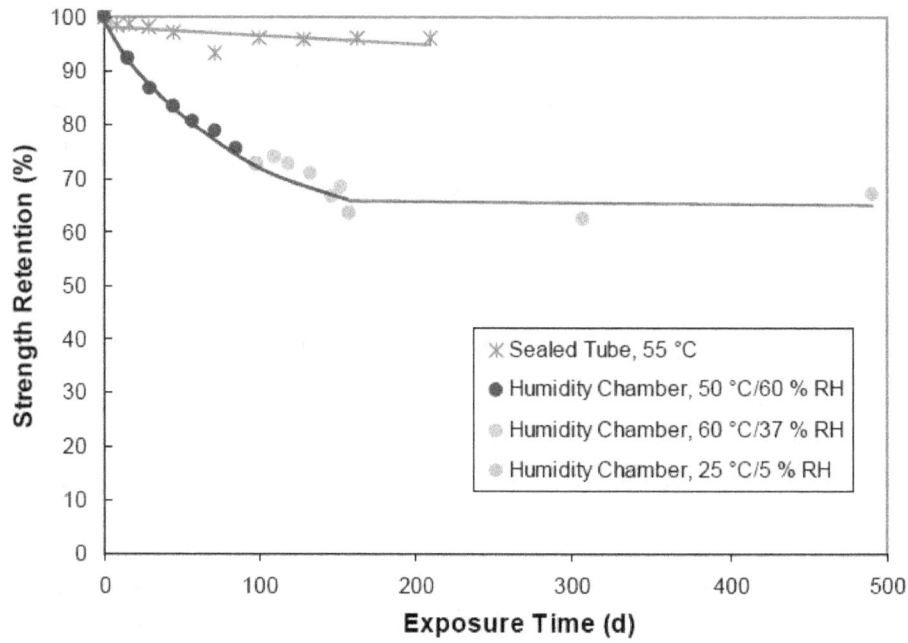

The sealed tube study confirms that PBO does not degrade under hot and dry conditions. The results indicate that if PBO is isolated from external sources of moisture, there is no significant change in its properties. This is a key finding because examinations of many used armor samples have revealed that most designs do little to protect the PBO from all forms of moisture. Traditionally, many armor models have used armor panel materials considered to be "waterproof," and their purpose was to lessen the amount of liquid water that could pass through the covering and into the ballistic materials. The Phase I and Phase II tests have revealed that many armor designs do not address the potential for water vapor transmission through the armor panel covering. Some armor models actually incorporate breathable membranes or fabrics that encourage the passage of humidity through the armor panel. Chemically, hydrolytic degradation would occur in the presence of either liquid water or water vapor.

U.S. Department of Justice
Office of Justice Programs
National Institute of Justice

Third Status Report to the Attorney General on
Body Armor Safety Initiative
Testing and Activities

F. Correlation of Chemical Changes to Mechanical Properties

Examination and comparison of the spectra from the various yarns in Figure 9 indicate that the degree of hydrolysis is greatest in the officer's armor, followed by the archive armor, and the least in the new armor, relative to the virgin yarn. This rank order follows the same rank order of tensile strength loss reported in Table 6. Tensile strength loss is therefore correlated with the degree of hydrolysis.

G. Degradation Mechanisms

Current data suggests that hydrolytic degradation in PBO may occur in two steps, with the first step resulting in the opening of the oxazole ring to form a new chemical structure that is similar to, but not the same as Kevlar (Figure 11). Kevlar is known to have tensile properties that are less than PBO, so it is reasonable to expect that this degradation product has mechanical properties that are less than PBO. This particular structure still forms a continuous, but weakened, polymer chain. The scientific literature also indicates that this degradation product could be further degraded in a second step by a complete breakage in the polymer chain. Establishing the extent of these two degradation steps will provide insight into the lower bound of the strength of PBO fiber under normal use conditions.

Figure 11. Chemical Structure of Kevlar, or poly(*p*-phenylene terephthalamide), repeat unit

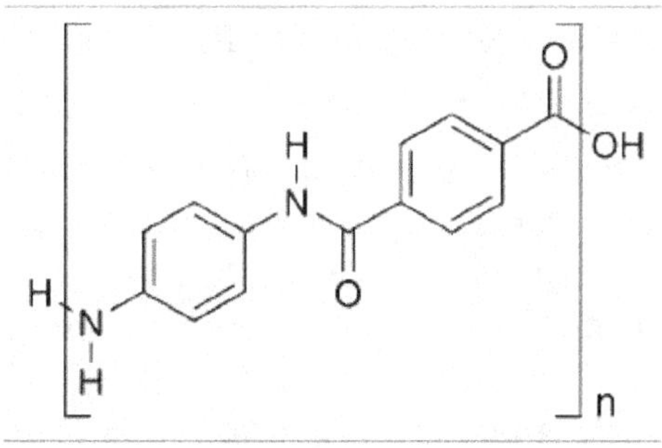

In the present study, the FTIR technique clearly reveals breakage of the oxazole ring and the formation of other chemical bonds that correspond to degradation products that appear in the chemical degradation pathway described in detail elsewhere[24]. In theoretical models of fiber

---

[24] Chin, J., et al., "Chemical Analysis of Poly(*p*-phenylene benzobisoxazole) Fibers Used in Ballistic Applications," NISTIR TBD (forthcoming) and Holmes, G.A., et al., "Ballistic Fibers: A Review of the Thermal, Ultraviolet and Hydrolytic Stability of the Benzoxazole Ring Structure," accepted for publication in the *Journal of Materials Science* (forthcoming).

U.S. Department of Justice
Office of Justice Programs
National Institute of Justice

Third Status Report to the Attorney General on
Body Armor Safety Initiative
Testing and Activities

tensile strength and modulus developed by Termonia et al.[25] and Jones and Martin,[26] both groups state that decreases in polymer chain length (i.e., breaking of the molecular bonds) are more detrimental to tensile strength than to elastic modulus. These observations are consistent with the armor yarn tensile properties reported in this study, in which degradation was observed in tensile strength but not elastic modulus. Preliminary investigations into PBO degradation mechanisms have suggested that oxazole ring breakage occurs as a result of both moisture and light exposures. Additional work is underway using model compounds to confirm these degradation theories and to study the sensitivity of PBO to other environments.

The presence of residual acid, left over from the original processing of the PBO fiber, has been alleged to cause degradation. Additional studies are underway to investigate the presence of residual acid and its role in degradation. Results of those studies will be presented in a future report.

VI.   Compliance Testing Process Review and Modifications

In his directive, the Attorney General charged NIJ with reviewing the existing process for compliance testing of body armor based on its research findings.

To respond to this directive, the U.S. Department of Justice convened a summit on March 11, 2004, to provide a forum for law enforcement, the scientific community, manufacturers, and other interested parties to discuss concerns with the reliability of body armor. Summit participants also examined the results of the ongoing testing of body armor systems containing Zylon®, the future of body armor technology and the current NIJ compliance testing process. Summit participants strongly recommended that NIJ revise its current compliance testing program to address the continued performance of body armor during its warranty period.

The current NIJ body armor standard is designed to assess the ballistic resistance of new armor systems. The standard does not include tests that address the ongoing performance of armor systems. The current process has adequately assessed the ballistic capabilities of new body armor systems—as demonstrated by the successful use of body armor over the past 30 years. However, the adequate performance of new armor is not, in and of itself, sufficient to ensure that the body armor actually being worn by officers will sufficiently protect them from death or serious injury. NIJ's research findings on Zylon® indicate that ongoing performance must be considered with body armor systems that contain materials whose physical properties degrade substantially as a result of environmental exposures.

---

[25] Y. Termonia, P. Meakin, and P. Smith, "Theoretical study of the influence of the molecular weight on the maximum tensile strength of polymer fibers." *Macromolecules*, 18, 2246-2252 (1985).

[26] M.-C. G. Jones and D.C. Martin, "Molecular stress and strain in an oriented extended-chain polymer of finite molecular length." *Macromolecules*, 28, 6161-6174 (1995).

U.S. Department of Justice
Office of Justice Programs
National Institute of Justice

Third Status Report to the Attorney General on
Body Armor Safety Initiative
Testing and Activities

Unfortunately, there are limited data concerning the ongoing performance of ballistic-resistant materials and associated armor systems currently in widespread use in the United States. Also, there is no accepted test protocol to evaluate the performance of used body armor over a period of years of typical law enforcement use. Future testing and research will support the development of a comprehensive and scientifically-rigorous compliance testing process designed to assure officers that their armor will continue to protect them over the armor's full warranty period.

In the meantime, NIJ will implement interim changes to its body armor compliance testing process. These interim changes create new requirements for all body armor manufacturers. However, manufacturers of Zylon®-based armor must satisfy additional requirements. They must affirmatively demonstrate to NIJ that their body armor will maintain its ballistic performance during the declared warranty period. Without such evidence, these body armors will not comply with the requirements of NIJ's body armor compliance testing program.

NIJ is continuing its comprehensive research to examine ballistic-resistant materials and improve our understanding of degradation mechanisms. As new information becomes available, NIJ will issue advisory notices to alert the public if any body armor materials appear to create a risk of death or serious injury as a result of degraded ballistic performance. Any body armor model that contains any material listed in such an advisory notice will be deemed no longer NIJ-compliant unless and until the manufacturer satisfies NIJ that the model will maintain its ballistic performance over its declared warranty period.

NIJ recommends that public safety agencies and officers purchase only bullet-resistant body armor models that comply with NIJ's new interim requirements, especially if their existing armor contains Zylon®. A list of models that comply with the requirements will be made available at http://www.justnet.org.

NIJ 2005 Interim Requirements for Bullet-Resistant Body Armor

The detailed provisions of the interim changes to the NIJ voluntary body armor compliance testing program will be as follows.

<u>Purpose and Scope</u>
These requirements modify and supplement National Institute of Justice (NIJ) Standard 0101.04 (Ballistic Resistance of Personal Body Armor). They are promulgated on an interim basis to address recent NIJ research findings that indicate that certain body armor models previously found by NIJ to be compliant with earlier NIJ requirements for ballistic resistance of new body armor (including NIJ Standard 0101.04) may not adequately maintain ballistic performance during their service life. In keeping with their interim character, these requirements rely in significant part on specific certifications from manufacturers of body armor. To help ensure the accuracy of the certifications, NIJ intends to implement a plan to conduct random or other assessments of the certifications and the evidence that underlies them. Also, in furtherance of

U.S. Department of Justice
Office of Justice Programs
National Institute of Justice

Third Status Report to the Attorney General on
Body Armor Safety Initiative
Testing and Activities

these efforts, from time to time, NIJ may issue Body Armor Standard Advisory Notices, among other things to identify to the public body armor materials that, based on NIJ review, appear to create a risk of death or serious injury as a result of degraded ballistic performance. Such Advisory Notices will be made available at: https://vests.ojp.gov/index.jsp.

NIJ recommends that those who purchase new bullet-resistant body armor after the effective date hereof select body armor models that comply with these interim requirements. A list of models that comply with these requirements will be made available at: http://www.justnet.org. NIJ will no longer publish lists of models found by NIJ (prior to the effective date hereof) to be compliant with earlier NIJ requirements for ballistic resistance of new body armor (including NIJ Standard 0101.04).

NIJ's efforts to ensure the safety of public safety officers are ongoing; NIJ intends to promulgate future modifications to these interim requirements as appropriate in light of its continued research and comments from the law enforcement and manufacturing communities. Comments and suggestions should be directed to the Director, Office of Science and Technology, National Institute of Justice, Office of Justice Programs, U.S. Department of Justice, 810 Seventh Street, N.W., Washington, D.C. 20531.

Requirements

Any body armor model submitted by a manufacturer to the NIJ Voluntary Compliance Testing Program on or after the effective date hereof or otherwise not subject to the Transition Provision (below) shall be subject to the following requirements:

1. Satisfaction, as determined by NIJ, of all of the requirements of NIJ Standard 0101.04 (including Addendum B), except as such requirements may be modified hereby;

2. Either –

   (a) Submission of evidence (*e.g.*, design drawings and specifications, lists of materials of construction of each component of the model, research, ballistic testing, descriptions of performance characteristics of critical components or materials, *etc.*) that demonstrates to the satisfaction of NIJ that the model will maintain ballistic performance (consistent with its originally declared threat level) over its declared warranty period; or

   (b) Submission, by an officer of the manufacturer who has the authority to bind it, of a written certification, the sufficiency of which shall be determined by NIJ, that –

      (1) The model contains no material listed in an NIJ Body Armor Standard Advisory Notice in effect at the time of submission;

U.S. Department of Justice
Office of Justice Programs
National Institute of Justice

Third Status Report to the Attorney General on
Body Armor Safety Initiative
Testing and Activities

    (2)   Lists the materials of construction of each component of the model;

    (3)   The officer, on behalf of the manufacturer –

        (A)   Reasonably believes that the model will maintain ballistic performance (consistent with its originally declared threat level) over its declared warranty period;

        (B)   Has objective evidence to support that belief; and

        (C)   Agrees to provide NIJ, promptly on demand, that evidence;

3.   Submission, by an officer of the manufacturer who has the authority to bind it, of a written certification, the sufficiency of which shall be determined by NIJ, that labeling of armor shall be in accordance with NIJ Standard 0101.04, except that any references to such standard thereon shall instead be to the "NIJ 2005 Interim Requirements"; and

4.   Submission, by an officer of the manufacturer who has the authority to bind it, of a written acknowledgment, the sufficiency of which shall be determined by NIJ, that –

    (a)   Recent NIJ research findings indicate that certain body armor models that were found by NIJ to be compliant with earlier NIJ requirements for ballistic resistance of new body armor (including NIJ Standard 0101.04) may not adequately maintain ballistic performance during their service life;

    (b)   NIJ recommends that those who purchase new bullet-resistant body armor select body armor models that comply with the NIJ 2005 Interim Requirements;

    (c)   NIJ will no longer publish lists of models found by NIJ to be compliant with earlier NIJ requirements for ballistic resistance of new body armor (including NIJ Standard 0101.04); and

    (d)   Any list or database of compliant body armor models published or sponsored by NIJ will include only models that are found by NIJ to comply with the NIJ 2005 Interim Requirements.

U.S. Department of Justice
Office of Justice Programs
National Institute of Justice

Third Status Report to the Attorney General on
Body Armor Safety Initiative
Testing and Activities

NIJ will issue to the manufacturer an NIJ Notice of Compliance upon determination that these Requirements have been satisfied.

<u>Transition Provision</u>
Any body armor model that was submitted by a manufacturer to NIJ and was found by NIJ to be compliant with NIJ Standard 0101.04 prior to the effective date hereof shall, if made by the same manufacturer, be deemed to comply with the NIJ 2005 Interim Requirements upon issuance to the manufacturer of an NIJ Notice of Compliance. To obtain an NIJ Notice of Compliance, the manufacturer shall submit, with respect to the body armor model –

1. Either –

    (a) The evidence described in Requirements ¶ 2(a); or

    (b) The certification described in Requirements ¶ 2(b)(1) & (2);

2. With respect to armor manufactured more than ten days after the date of the NIJ Notice of Compliance, the certification described in Requirements ¶ 3; and

3. The acknowledgment described in Requirements ¶ 4.

In the event the manufacturer submits a certification pursuant to this Transition Provision ¶ 1(b), the manufacturer also must submit to NIJ, within 90 days of the date of the NIJ Notice of Compliance, the certification described in Requirements ¶ 2(b)(3); if the manufacturer fails to submit this certification, the body armor model shall be deemed no longer to be in compliance with the NIJ 2005 Interim Requirements (and shall be removed from any NIJ list of models that comply with the Requirements) until the manufacturer submits it and NIJ issues a new NIJ Notice of Compliance.

<u>Loss of Compliance Status</u>
A body armor model that is the subject of an NIJ Notice of Compliance shall be deemed no longer to be in compliance with the NIJ 2005 Interim Requirements (and shall be removed from any NIJ list of models that comply with the Requirements) if –

1. NIJ issues an NIJ Body Armor Standard Advisory Notice that identifies a material contained in the model;

2. NIJ determines that any certification or acknowledgment submitted with respect to the model is insufficient or inaccurate;

3. The manufacturer fails to provide NIJ promptly on demand the evidence described in Requirements ¶ 2(b)(3); or

U.S. Department of Justice
Office of Justice Programs
National Institute of Justice

Third Status Report to the Attorney General on
Body Armor Safety Initiative
Testing and Activities

4. NIJ determines, at any time, that the evidence provided to NIJ as described in Requirements ¶ 2(b)(3) and/or in connection with the model is insufficient to demonstrate to the satisfaction of NIJ that the model will maintain its ballistic performance (consistent with its originally declared threat level) over its declared warranty period.

Once a body armor model loses compliance status under this provision, the model will remain out of compliance unless and until NIJ issues a new NIJ Notice of Compliance, following the submission of such evidence (*e.g.*, evidence described in Requirements ¶ 2(a)), documentation, information, or other material as NIJ may require.

Labeling after Loss of Compliance Status
Armor manufactured during a period in which the armor model does not comply (or is deemed not to comply) with the NIJ 2005 Interim Requirements shall not be labeled as compliant with them.

VII. Summary

Body armor manufacturers must consider a number of competing requirements when they design an armor system that will maintain the intended level of ballistic resistance over time. Armor designers face demands to satisfy performance and operational requirements, while making the armor more comfortable by making it thinner, lighter, and cooler. It is critical for the armor design to anticipate potential changes that may occur in the armor during field use, because of the potential for those changes to affect adversely the ballistic performance of the armor. Users of body armor also have a responsibility to properly care for and maintain their body armor to reduce the potential for inadvertent damage to the armor.

There are hundreds of possible combinations of materials, weave patterns, stitching details, layer counts, and ply lay-ups that could be used to produce a body armor design that initially meets the requirements of the NIJ standard. Manufacturers are responsible for building an extra performance margin into their design. Because there are market incentives for building armor models that are thinner, lighter, and more breathable, the safety margins in armors may vary. The Zylon® fiber is susceptible to hydrolytic (moisture) and photolytic (light) degradation. Published scientific literature confirms these degradation mechanisms. Any armor design relying on Zylon® must take into account these susceptibilities and the resulting reduction in mechanical properties and ballistic performance. Based on test results of used armor, if Zylon® material is being relied upon to contribute ballistic resistance to body armor, then the body armor may not maintain the intended level of ballistic resistance.

The findings from ballistic testing and applied research have led to a better understanding of armor degradation mechanisms in Zylon® and other ballistic resistant materials, as well as the correlation between certain material properties and ballistic performance. These findings will also assist in the development of modifications to the existing body armor standard and

U.S. Department of Justice
Office of Justice Programs
National Institute of Justice

Third Status Report to the Attorney General on
Body Armor Safety Initiative
Testing and Activities

compliance testing process, especially as it relates to test methods to ensure the ongoing performance of used body armor.

In the meantime, NIJ will issue the NIJ 2005 Interim Requirements for Bullet-Resistant Body Armor discussed in Section VI of this report. NIJ strongly recommends that those public safety agencies who purchase new bullet-resistant body armor select models that comply with these interim requirements. A list of compliant body armor models can be found at http://www.justnet.org.

NIJ continues to strongly encourage public safety officers to wear their Zylon®-containing body armor until it can be replaced.

Appendix A. Complete Results of Phase I (Worst Case) P-BFS Test

Level IIA Armor, Compliant to NIJ-0101.03

Sample	OLES ID Number	Panel Tested	Manufacturer	Model Number	Material	Date of Issue / Manufacture	Age (months)	Armor Condition	Pen 9 mm (note 1) 1st 0°	2nd 0°	30°	Pen 357 Mag (note 2) 1st 0°	2nd 0°	30°	Result	BFS 9 mm 1st 0°	2nd 0°	BFS 357 Mag 1st 0°	2nd 0°	Result
1	UZ016	Front	SCBA	ZYL-IIA 898101	All Zylon	July-2001	31	4	No	No	No	No	No	No	Pass	48	44	51	55	Fail
2	UZ021	Front	SCBA	ZYL-IIA 898101	All Zylon	September-2000	41	3	No	No	No	No	No	No	Pass	51	44	55	54	Fail
3	UZ028	Front	SCBA	ZYL-IIA 898101	All Zylon	March-1999	59	3	No	No	No	Yes	Yes	No	Fail	48	47	N/A	N/A	N/A

Level II Armor, Compliant to NIJ-0101.03

Sample	OLES ID Number	Panel Tested	Manufacturer	Model Number	Material	Date of Issue / Manufacture	Age (months)	Armor Condition	Pen 9 mm (note 3) 1st 0°	2nd 0°	30°	Pen 357 Mag (note 4) 1st 0°	2nd 0°	30°	Result	BFS 9 mm 1st 0°	2nd 0°	BFS 357 Mag 1st 0°	2nd 0°	Result
1	UZ029	Front	SCBA	AZG-II 995120	Zylon Hybrid	June-2002	20	3	No	No	No	No	No	No	Pass	43	44	48	55	Fail
2	UZ003	Front	SCBA	ZYL-II 898101	All Zylon	September-2000	41	4	No	No	No	No	Yes	No	Fail	45	46	46	N/A	N/A
3	UZ015	Front	SCBA	ZYL-II 898101	All Zylon	July-1999	55	3	No	No	No	Yes	Yes	No	Fail	41	45	N/A	N/A	N/A
4	UZ020	Front	SCBA	ZYL-II 898101	All Zylon	June-2000	44	3	No	No	No	No	Yes	No	Fail	49	51	49	N/A	N/A
5	UZ024	Front	SCBA	ZYL-II 898101	All Zylon	July-1999	55	3	No	No	No	Yes	Yes	Yes	Fail	47	46	N/A	N/A	N/A

Level II Armor, Compliant to NIJ-0101.04

Sample	OLES ID Number	Panel Tested	Manufacturer	Model Number	Material	Date of Issue / Manufacture	Age (months)	Armor Condition	Pen 9 mm (note 3) 1st 0°	2nd 0°	30°	Pen 357 Mag (note 4) 1st 0°	2nd 0°	30°	Result	BFS 9 mm 1st 0°	2nd 0°	BFS 357 Mag 1st 0°	2nd 0°	Result
1	UZ017	Front	PT Armor	PTZG2	Zylon Hybrid	April-2002	22	3	No	No	No	No	No	No	Pass	35	39	35	43	*Pass*
2	UZ027	Front	PT Armor	PTZG2	Zylon Hybrid	February-2002	24	2	No	No	No	No	No	No	Pass	37	37	40	45	Fail
3	UZ002	Front	SCBA	SMU-II+ 001221	All Zylon	September-2001	29	3	No	No	No	Yes	Yes	Yes	Fail	32	35	40	N/A	N/A
4	UZ018	Front	SCBA	SMU-II+ 001221	All Zylon	February-2003	12	2	No	No	No	Yes	Yes	No	Fail	34	37	43	N/A	N/A
5	UZ006	Front	ABA	XTX2-1	Zylon Hybrid	September-2003	9	2	No	No	No	No	No	No	Pass	35	32	40	58	Fail
6	UZ008	Front	ABA	XTX2-1	Zylon Hybrid	August-2002	22	3	No	No	No	Yes	No	No	Fail	35	38	N/A	76	N/A
7	UZ009	Front	ABA	XTX2-1	Zylon Hybrid	June-2002	24	3	No	No	No	Yes	Yes	No	Fail	33	57	N/A	N/A	N/A
8	UZ014	Front	ABA	XTX2-1	Zylon Hybrid	February-2003	12	3	No	No	No	No	Yes	No	Fail	36	35	46	46	Fail
9	UZ022	Front	ABA	XTX2-1	Zylon Hybrid	April-2002	22	3	No	No	No	No	No	No	Pass	36	33	40	N/A	N/A
10	UZ023	Front	ABA	XTZX2-1	Zylon Hybrid	#N/A	unknown	3	No	Yes	No	No	Yes	Yes	Fail	37	N/A	48	42	*Pass*
11	UZ007	Front	Gall's	ZL2-2	Zylon Hybrid	#N/A	unknown	2	No	No	No	No	No	No	Pass	30	36	42	42	Pass
12	UZ004	Front	PT Armor	ZX-2	Zylon Hybrid	February-2004	3	1	No	No	No	No	No	No	Pass	32	39	40	47	Fail
13	UZ005	Front	PT Armor	ZX-2	Zylon Hybrid	June-2003	11	3	No	No	No	No	No	No	Pass	32	43	51	58	Fail

Level IIIA Armor, Compliant to NIJ-0101.03

Sample	OLES ID Number	Panel Tested	Manufacturer	Model Number	Material	Date of Issue / Manufacture	Age (months)	Armor Condition	Pen 9 mm (note 5) 1st 0°	2nd 0°	30°	Pen 44 Mag (note 6) 1st 0°	2nd 0°	30°	Result	BFS 9 mm 1st 0°	2nd 0°	BFS 44 Mag 1st 0°	2nd 0°	Result
1	UZ025	Front	SCBA	ZYL-IIIA 898101	All Zylon	August-2001	30	4	No	No	No	No	Yes	No	Fail	50	45	68	N/A	N/A

Level IIIA Armor, Compliant to NIJ-0101.04

Sample	OLES ID Number	Panel Tested	Manufacturer	Model Number	Material	Date of Issue / Manufacture	Age (months)	Armor Condition	Pen 9 mm (note 5) 1st 0°	2nd 0°	30°	Pen 44 Mag (note 6) 1st 0°	2nd 0°	30°	Result	BFS 9 mm 1st 0°	2nd 0°	BFS 44 Mag 1st 0°	2nd 0°	Result
1	UZ030	Front	P.A.C.A.	04ZPG3A-1	Zylon Hybrid	July-2003	11	2	No	No	No	No	No	No	Pass	23	31	46	52	Fail
2	UZ031	Front	P.A.C.A.	04ZPG3A-1	Zylon Hybrid	February-2004	4	1	No	No	No	No	No	No	Pass	31	31	43	48	Fail
3	UZ010	Front	Point Blank	F-13-5	Zylon Hybrid	January-2000	53	2	No	No	No	No	No	No	Pass	30	28	43	63	Fail
4	UZ011	Front	Point Blank	F-13-5	Zylon Hybrid	#N/A	unknown	2	No	No	No	No	No	No	Pass	32	31	42	45	Fail
5	UZ019	Front	SCBA	SMU-IIIA+ FEM 109040	All Zylon	June-2003	8	2	No	No	No	No	No	No	Pass	39	43	56	55	Fail
6	UZ026	Front	Point Blank	ZL6	Zylon Hybrid	#N/A	unknown	2	No	No	No	No	No	No	Pass	39	35	43	52	Fail

Notes:
1) The 9 mm threats for level IIA armor are a 124 gr. 9 mm FMJ RN bullet with a velocity of 1090 (+50/-0) ft/s for NIJ 0101.03 armor and a velocity of 1120 (±30) ft/s for NIJ 0101.04 armor.
2) The magnum threats for level IIA armor are a 158 gr. 357 Magnum JSP bullet at 1250 (+50/-0) ft/s for NIJ 0101.03 armor and a 180 gr. 40 S&W FMJ bullet at 1055 (±30) ft/s for NIJ 0101.04 armor.
3) The 9 mm threats for level II armor are a 124 gr. 9 mm FMJ RN bullet with a velocity of 1175 (+50/-0) ft/s for NIJ 0101.03 armor and a velocity of 1205 (±30) ft/s for NIJ 0101.04 armor.
4) The magnum threats for level II armor are a 158 gr. 357 Magnum JSP bullet with a velocity of 1395 (+50/-0) ft/s for NIJ 0101.03 armor and a velocity of 1430 (±30) ft/s for NIJ 0101.04 armor.
5) The 9 mm threats for level IIIA armor are a 124 gr. 9 mm FMJ RN bullet with a velocity of 1400 (+50/-0) ft/s for NIJ 0101.03 armor and a velocity of 1430 (±30) ft/s for NIJ 0101.04 armor.
6) The magnum threats for level IIIA armor are a 240 gr. 44 Mag LSWCGC bullet at 1400 (+50/-0) ft/s for NIJ 0101.03 armor and a 240 gr. 44 Mag SJHP bullet at 1430 (±30) ft/s for NIJ 0101.04 armor.
7) The armor condition refers to a visual inspection. Condition 1 refers to armor that shows no visible signs of wear and is in new or "like new" condition. Condition 2 refers to armor that shows light to moderate signs of wear. Condition 3 refers to armor that shows significant signs of wear (daily use for extended period). Condition 4 refers to armor that shows signs of extreme wear or abuse.

Appendix B. Phase I (Worst Case) Ballistic Limit and Tensile Strength Test Results

Level IIA Armor, Compliant to NIJ-0101.03

Sample	OLES ID Number	Manufacturer	Model Number	Material	NIJ Max Ref Vel (ft/s)	Compliance V50 (ft/s)	Armor V50 (ft/s)	V50 Diff. (ft/s)	V50 - Ref (ft/s)	Percent Decline[3]	New Yarn (GPa)	Vest Average (GPa)	Strength Loss (GPa)	Strength Loss (%)
1	UZ016	SCBA	ZYL-IIA 898101	All Zylon	1140	-	1350	-	210	-	4.78	2.20	2.59	54%
2	UZ021	SCBA	ZYL-IIA 898101	All Zylon	1140	-	1352	-	212	-	4.78	2.43	2.35	49%
3	UZ028	SCBA	ZYL-IIA 898101	All Zylon	1140	-	1169	-	29	-	4.78	1.87	2.91	61%

Level II Armor, Compliant to NIJ-0101.03

Sample	OLES ID Number	Manufacturer	Model Number	Material	NIJ Max Ref Vel (ft/s)	Compliance V50 (ft/s)	Armor V50 (ft/s)	V50 Diff. (ft/s)	V50 - Ref (ft/s)	Percent Decline[3]	New Yarn (GPa)	Vest Average (GPa)	Strength Loss (GPa)	Strength Loss (%)
1	UZ029	SCBA	AZG-II 995120	Zylon Hybrid	1225	-	1644	-	419	-	4.78	3.34	1.44	30%
2	UZ003	SCBA	ZYL-II 898101	All Zylon	1225	-	1438	-	213	-	4.78	2.18	2.60	54%
3	UZ015	SCBA	ZYL-II 898101	All Zylon	1225	-	1355	-	130	-	4.78	1.87	2.91	61%
4	UZ020	SCBA	ZYL-II 898101	All Zylon	1225	-	1363	-	138	-	4.78	1.98	2.80	59%
5	UZ024	SCBA	ZYL-II 898101	All Zylon	1225	-	1362	-	137	-	4.78	2.35	2.43	51%

Level II Armor, Compliant to NIJ-0101.04

Sample	OLES ID Number	Manufacturer	Model Number	Material	NIJ Max Ref Vel (ft/s)	Compliance V50 (ft/s)	Armor V50 (ft/s)	V50 Diff. (ft/s)	V50 - Ref (ft/s)	Percent Decline[3]	New Yarn (GPa)	Vest Average (GPa)	Strength Loss (GPa)	Strength Loss (%)
1	UZ017	PT Armor	PTZG2	Zylon Hybrid	1235	1590	1493	-97	258	27%	4.78	2.85	1.93	40%
2	UZ027	PT Armor	PTZG2	Zylon Hybrid	1235	1590	1531	-59	296	17%	4.78	2.82	1.97	41%
3	UZ002	SCBA	SMU-II+ 001221	All Zylon	1235	1703	1423	-280	188	60%	4.78	2.49	2.30	48%
4	UZ018	SCBA	SMU-II+ 001221	All Zylon	1235	1703	1490	-213	255	46%	4.78	3.08	1.70	36%
5	UZ006	ABA	XTX2-1	Zylon Hybrid	1235	1608	1498	-110	263	29%	4.78	3.82	0.97	20%
6	UZ008	ABA	XTX2-1	Zylon Hybrid	1235	1608	1477	-131	242	35%	4.78	3.34	1.44	30%
7	UZ009	ABA	XTX2-1	Zylon Hybrid	1235	1608	1451	-157	216	42%	4.78	2.72	2.06	43%
8	UZ014	ABA	XTX2-1	Zylon Hybrid	1235	1608	1417	-191	182	51%	4.78	3.09	1.70	35%
9	UZ022	ABA	XTX2-1	Zylon Hybrid	1235	1608	1519	-89	284	24%	4.78	3.36	1.43	30%
10	UZ023	ABA	XTZX2-1	Zylon Hybrid	1235	1554	1264	-290	29	91%	4.78	2.85	1.94	40%
11	UZ007	Gall's	ZL2-2	Zylon Hybrid	1235	1568	1474	-94	239	28%	4.78	4.26	0.52	11%
12	UZ004	PT Armor	ZX-2	Zylon Hybrid	1235	1543	1617	74	382	Increased	-	-	-	-
13	UZ005	PT Armor	ZX-2	Zylon Hybrid	1235	1543	1547	4	312	Increased	-	-	-	-

Level IIIA Armor, Compliant to NIJ-0101.03

Sample	OLES ID Number	Manufacturer	Model Number	Material	NIJ Max Ref Vel (ft/s)	Compliance V50 (ft/s)	Armor V50 (ft/s)	V50 Diff. (ft/s)	V50 - Ref (ft/s)	Percent Decline[3]	New Yarn (GPa)	Vest Average (GPa)	Strength Loss (GPa)	Strength Loss (%)
1	UZ025	SCBA	ZYL-IIIA 898101	All Zylon	1450	-	1457	-	7	-	4.78	2.22	2.56	54%

Level IIIA Armor, Compliant to NIJ-0101.04

Sample	OLES ID Number	Manufacturer	Model Number	Material	NIJ Max Ref Vel (ft/s)	Compliance V50 (ft/s)	Armor V50 (ft/s)	V50 Diff. (ft/s)	V50 - Ref (ft/s)	Percent Decline[3]	New Yarn (GPa)	Vest Average (GPa)	Strength Loss (GPa)	Strength Loss (%)
1	UZ030	P.A.C.A.	04ZPG3A-1	Zylon Hybrid	1460	1752	1679	-73	219	25%	-	-	-	-
2	UZ031	P.A.C.A.	04ZPG3A-1	Zylon Hybrid	1460	1752	1684	-68	224	23%	-	-	-	-
3	UZ010	Point Blank	F13-5	Zylon Hybrid	1460	1859	1766	-93	306	23%	-	-	-	-
4	UZ011	Point Blank	F13-5	Zylon Hybrid	1460	1859	1783	-76	323	19%	-	-	-	-
5	UZ019	SCBA	SMU-IIIA+ FEM 109040	All Zylon	1460	1863	1699	-164	239	41%	4.78	3.38	1.41	29%
6	UZ026	Point Blank	ZL6	Zylon Hybrid	1460	1684	1561	-123	101	55%	4.78	3.39	1.39	29%

Notes:

1) The ballistic limit tests were performed on the rear panels of each armor.

2) The tensile tests were performed on yarns extracted from the front panel of each armor.

3) The ballistic limit "Percent Decline" is calculated as the decline in the V50 value divided by the difference between the compliance V50 and he maximum NIJ reference velocity. Thus, a 100% V50 decline will correspond to a used armor V50 that has declined to the maximum NIJ reference velocity.

Appendix C. Results of Phase II P-BFS Testing

Level IIA Armor, Compliant to NIJ-0101.03

Sample	OLES ID Number	Panel Tested	Manufacturer	Model Number	Material	Date of Issue / Manufacture	Age (months)	Armor Condition	Penetrations 9 mm (see note 1) 1st 0°	2nd 0°	30°	357 Mag (see note 2) 1st 0°	2nd 0°	30°	Result	Back Face Signature 9 mm 1st 0°	2nd 0°	357 Mag 1st 0°	2nd 0°	Result
1	UZ035	Back	SCBA	AZG-IIA 896280	Zylon Hybrid	May-2000	61	4	Yes	Yes	Yes	Yes	Yes	Yes	Fail	N/A	N/A	N/A	N/A	N/A
2	UZ041	Front	SCBA	ZYL-IIA 898101	All Zylon	May-2000	61	4	Yes	No	Yes	No	No	No	Fail	N/A	66	58	57	N/A
3	UZ058	Front	SCBA	ZYL-IIA 898101	All Zylon	January-2000	65	4	No	Yes	Yes	No	No	No	Fail	50	N/A	66	58	N/A

Level IIA Armor, Compliant to NIJ-0101.04

Sample	OLES ID Number	Panel Tested	Manufacturer	Model Number	Material	Date of Issue / Manufacture	Age (months)	Armor Condition	Penetrations 9 mm (see note 1) 1st 0°	2nd 0°	30°	40 S&W (see note 2) 1st 0°	2nd 0°	30°	Result	Back Face Signature 9 mm 1st 0°	2nd 0°	40 S&W 1st 0°	2nd 0°	Result
1	UZ083	Back	First Choice	MSF-IIA	All Zylon	April-2003	26	3	No	No	No	No	No	No	Fail	39	42	N/A	44	N/A
2	UZ034	Front	SCBA	SMU-IIA +105130	All Zylon	June-2001	48	4	No	No	No	No	No	No	Pass	48	44	49	52	Fail
3	UZ056	Back	PACA	ZPG IIA	Zylon Hybrid	June-2001	48	4	Yes	Yes	Yes	No	No	No	Fail	N/A	N/A	60	45	N/A

Level II Armor, Compliant to NIJ-0101.03

Sample	OLES ID Number	Panel Tested	Manufacturer	Model Number	Material	Date of Issue / Manufacture	Age (months)	Armor Condition	Penetrations 9 mm (see note 3) 1st 0°	2nd 0°	30°	357 Mag (see note 4) 1st 0°	2nd 0°	30°	Result	Back Face Signature 9 mm 1st 0°	2nd 0°	357 Mag 1st 0°	2nd 0°	Result
1	UZ051	Front	SCBA	AZG-II 995120	Zylon Hybrid	November-2000	54	3	No	No	Yes	Yes	No	No	Fail	45	48	N/A	47	N/A
2	UZ052	Back	SCBA	AZG-II 995120	Zylon Hybrid	October-2001	43	4	-	Yes	Yes	-	Yes	Yes	Fail	-	N/A	N/A	N/A	N/A
3	UZ063	Front	SCBA	AZG-II 995120	Zylon Hybrid	August-2001	45	3	-	Yes	Yes	Yes	Yes	Yes	Fail	-	N/A	N/A	N/A	N/A
4	UZ074	Back	SCBA	AZG-II 995120	Zylon Hybrid	January-2003	27	3	Yes	Yes	Yes	Yes	Yes	-	Fail	N/A	N/A	N/A	N/A	N/A
5	UZ082	Back	SCBA	AZG-II 995120	Zylon Hybrid	July-2002	35	4	Yes	Yes	Yes	Yes	Yes	Yes	Fail	N/A	N/A	N/A	N/A	N/A
6	UZ092	Back	SCBA	AZG-II 995120	Zylon Hybrid	May-2002	37	3	Yes	Yes	Yes	Yes	Yes	Yes	Fail	N/A	N/A	N/A	N/A	N/A
7	UZ094	Front	SCBA	AZG-II 995120	Zylon Hybrid	July-2000	59	4	Yes	Yes	Yes	Yes	Yes	Yes	Fail	N/A	N/A	N/A	N/A	N/A
8	UZ095	Back	SCBA	AZG-II 995120	Zylon Hybrid	September-2000	56	4	Yes	Yes	Yes	Yes	Yes	Yes	Fail	N/A	N/A	N/A	N/A	N/A
9	UZ096	Back	SCBA	AZG-II 995120	Zylon Hybrid	September-2000	56	4	Yes	Yes	Yes	Yes	Yes	Yes	Fail	N/A	N/A	N/A	N/A	N/A
10	UZ097	Front	SCBA	AZG-II 995120	Zylon Hybrid	September-2000	56	4	Yes	Yes	Yes	Yes	Yes	Yes	Fail	N/A	N/A	N/A	N/A	N/A
11	UZ036	Back	First Choice	MF2000	All Zylon	July-2001	46	3	No	No	No	No	No	No	Pass	45	46	54	51	Fail
12	UZ042	Front	First Choice	MF2000	All Zylon	August-2001	45	3	No	No	No	No	No	No	Pass	47	47	61	49	Fail
13	UZ043	Front	First Choice	MF2000	All Zylon	August-2001	45	3	No	No	No	No	No	No	Pass	49	42	55	53	Fail
14	UZ059	Back	First Choice	MF2000	All Zylon	November-2001	42	3	No	No	No	No	No	No	Pass	41	-	68	55	N/A
15	UZ071	Back	First Choice	MF2000	All Zylon	August-2001	45	4	No	Yes	No	Yes	No	Yes	Fail	48	46	N/A	58	N/A
16	UZ072	Front	First Choice	MF2000	All Zylon	July-2000	58	3	No	No	No	No	No	Yes	Fail	50	48	50	N/A	N/A
17	UZ065	Back	PPI	Z-22	All Zylon	July-2001	46	2	No	No	No	Yes	No	No	Fail	38	38	N/A	54	N/A
18	UZ066	Front	PPI	Z-22	All Zylon	July-2001	46	2	No	No	No	No	Yes	Yes	Fail	42	37	53	N/A	N/A
19	UZ067	Front	PPI	Z-22	All Zylon	July-2001	46	3	No	No	No	Yes	Yes	Yes	Fail	39	40	N/A	N/A	N/A
20	UZ085	Front	PPI	Z-22	All Zylon	May-2001	49	3	No	No	No	Yes	Yes	No	Fail	49	38	N/A	N/A	N/A
21	UZ086	Front	PPI	Z-22	All Zylon	May-2001	48	3	No	No	No	No	No	No	Fail	42	36	50	53	N/A
22	UZ087	Back	PPI	Z-22	All Zylon	May-2001	48	3	Yes	Yes	Yes	Yes	Yes	Yes	Fail	N/A	35	N/A	N/A	N/A
23	UZ088	Back	PPI	Z-22	All Zylon	April-2001	50	4	No	No	No	No	Yes	No	Fail	41	30	47	-	N/A
24	UZ089	Front	PPI	Z-22	All Zylon	April-2001	49	3	No	No	No	No	No	No	Fail	35	41	53	-	N/A
25	UZ090	Back	PPI	Z-22	All Zylon	May-2001	49	2	No	Yes	No	No	No	No	Fail	38	N/A	53	60	N/A
26	UZ032	Front	SCBA	ZYL-II 898101	All Zylon	September-2000	56	2	No	No	No	No	No	No	Pass	49	45	65	60	Fail
27	UZ033	Back	SCBA	ZYL-II 898101	All Zylon	September-2000	56	2	No	No	No	No	No	No	Pass	46	47	52	55	Fail
28	UZ040	Front	SCBA	ZYL-II 898101	All Zylon	May-2000	60	4	No	No	No	No	Yes	No	Fail	49	43	62	N/A	N/A
29	UZ047	Back	SCBA	ZYL-II 898101	All Zylon	August-1999	69	4	No	No	No	No	No	No	Pass	51	44	66	-	N/A
30	UZ050	Front	SCBA	ZYL-II 898101	All Zylon	April-2000	61	3	Yes	Yes	Yes	Yes	Yes	Yes	Fail	44	42	N/A	54	N/A
31	UZ054	Back	SCBA	ZYL-II 898101	All Zylon	May-2000	60	4	Yes	No	No	Yes	No	No	Fail	47	48	N/A	56	N/A
32	UZ064	Back	SCBA	ZYL-II 898101	All Zylon	November-1999	66	2	No	No	No	No	No	No	Pass	47	-	55	55	Fail

Level II Armor, Compliant to NIJ-0101.04

Sample	OLES ID Number	Panel Tested	Manufacturer	Model Number	Material	Date of Issue / Manufacture	Age (months)	Armor Condition	Penetrations 9 mm (see note 3) 1st 0°	2nd 0°	30°	357 Mag (see note 4) 1st 0°	2nd 0°	30°	Result	BFS 9 mm 1st 0°	2nd 0°	357 Mag 1st 0°	2nd 0°	Result
1	UZ037	Back	Gator Hawk	GH-2-1023	Zylon Hybrid	July-2002	33	4	No	No	No	No	No	Yes	Fail	40	40	55	46	N/A
2	UZ091	Front	Gator Hawk	GH-2-1023	Zylon Hybrid	July-2002	34	4	No	No	No	No	No	No	Pass	40	38	52	45	Fail
3	UZ093	Back	Gator Hawk	GH-2-1023	Zylon Hybrid	September-2002	32	4	No	No	No	No	No	No	Pass	41	38	50	44	Fail
4	UZ045	Front	SCBA	SMU-II+001221	All Zylon	August-2002	33	3	No	No	No	No	No	No	Pass	47	35	53	54	Fail
5	UZ055	Front	SCBA	SMU-II+001221	All Zylon	January-2002	39	3	No	Yes	No	No	No	No	Pass	39	39	48	48	Fail
6	UZ061	Front	ABA	XTX2-1	Zylon Hybrid	May-2002	36	3	No	No	No	Yes	No	Yes	Fail	45	N/A	N/A	62	N/A
7	UZ068	Back	ABA	XTX2-1	Zylon Hybrid	June-2001	47	4	No	No	No	Yes	No	Yes	Fail	44	34	N/A	50	N/A
8	UZ073	Front	ABA	XTX2-1	Zylon Hybrid	March-2003	26	3	No	No	No	No	No	No	Pass	35	33	45	44	Fail
9	UZ078	Front	ABA	XTX2-1	Zylon Hybrid	December-2002	29	3	No	No	No	Yes	No	Yes	Fail	35	39	N/A	45	N/A
10	UZ038	Back	ABA	XTZX2-1	Zylon Hybrid	June-2001	47	2	No	No	No	Yes	Yes	Yes	Fail	43	44	N/A	N/A	N/A
11	UZ039	Back	ABA	XTZX2-1	Zylon Hybrid	June-2001	47	3	No	No	Yes	Yes	Yes	Yes	Fail	N/A	35	N/A	N/A	N/A
12	UZ081	Front	ABA	XTZX2-1	Zylon Hybrid	June-2003	23	4	Yes	No	Yes	Yes	Yes	–	Fail	N/A	49	N/A	N/A	N/A
13	UZ108	Back	ABA	XTZX2-1	Zylon Hybrid	#N/A	unknown	4	Yes	Yes	Yes	Yes	Yes	Yes	Fail	N/A	N/A	45	43	Fail
14	UZ110	Back	PACA	ZGII	Zylon Hybrid	January-2004	17	2	No	No	No	No	No	No	Fail	32	28	50	N/A	N/A
15	UZ062	Back	Point Blank	ZL5	Zylon Hybrid	#N/A	unknown	3	No	No	No	No	Yes	Yes	Fail	37	36	53	45	Fail
16	UZ084	Back	Point Blank	ZL5	Zylon Hybrid	#N/A	unknown	3	No	No	No	No	No	No	Pass	36	44	38	47	Fail
17	UZ109	Front	Point Blank	ZL5	Zylon Hybrid	#N/A	unknown	3	Yes	No	No	No	No	No	Pass	38	26			

Level IIIA Armor, Compliant to NIJ-0101.03

Sample	OLES ID Number	Panel Tested	Manufacturer	Model Number	Material	Date of Issue / Manufacture	Age (months)	Armor Condition	Penetrations 9 mm (see note 5) 1st 0°	2nd 0°	30°	44 Mag (see note 6) 1st 0°	2nd 0°	30°	Result	BFS 9 mm 1st 0°	2nd 0°	44 Mag 1st 0°	2nd 0°	Result
1	UZ048	Front	SCBA	AZG-IIIA 896280	Zylon Hybrid	January-2002	41	4	Yes	Yes	Yes	Yes	Yes	Yes	Fail	N/A	N/A	91	N/A	N/A
2	UZ057	Back	SCBA	AZG-IIIA 896280	Zylon Hybrid	February-2000	64	4	No	No	No	No	No	No	Pass	40	38	48	48	Fail
3	UZ106	Front	SCBA	AZG-IIIA 896280	Zylon Hybrid	October-2000	56	3	No	No	No	No	No	No	Pass	44	42	53	49	Fail
4	UZ100	Back	Point Blank	F04-1	Zylon Hybrid	November-2000	55	4	No	No	No	No	No	No	Pass	27	24	40	40	Pass
5	UZ101	Front	Point Blank	F04-1	Zylon Hybrid	November-2000	55	4	No	No	No	No	No	No	Pass	30	29	45	36	Fail
6	UZ102	Front	Point Blank	F04-1	Zylon Hybrid	November-2000	55	3	No	No	No	No	No	No	Pass	29	27	44	43	Pass
7	UZ103	Back	Point Blank	F04-1	Zylon Hybrid	November-2000	55	4	No	No	No	No	No	No	Pass	30	22	38	47	Fail
8	UZ044	Front	SCBA	ZYL-IIIA 898101	All Zylon	July-1999	71	4	No	No	No	No	No	No	Fail	49	54	75	67	Fail
9	UZ104	Back	SCBA	ZYL-IIIA 898101	All Zylon	January-2000	65	3	No	Yes	No	No	Yes	No	Fail	43	N/A	70	N/A	N/A
10	UZ105	Back	SCBA	ZYL-IIIA 898101	All Zylon	September-1999	69	4	Yes	Yes	No	Yes	No	No	Fail	N/A	56	80		N/A

Level IIIA Armor, Compliant to NIJ-0101.04

Sample	OLES ID Number	Panel Tested	Manufacturer	Model Number	Material	Date of Issue / Manufacture	Age (months)	Armor Condition	Penetrations 9 mm (see note 5) 1st 0°	2nd 0°	30°	44 Mag (see note 6) 1st 0°	2nd 0°	30°	Result	BFS 9 mm 1st 0°	2nd 0°	44 Mag 1st 0°	2nd 0°	Result
1	UZ107	Front	First Choice	MF733	Zylon Hybrid	June-2002	36	2	No	No	No	Yes	No	No	Fail	36	32	N/A	49	N/A
2	UZ060	Back	ABA	XTX3A-1	Zylon Hybrid	#N/A	unknown	4	Yes	Yes	Yes	Yes	Yes	Yes	Fail	N/A	N/A	N/A	N/A	N/A
3	UZ069	Back	ABA	XTX3A-1	Zylon Hybrid	September-2001	45	3	Yes	No	No	Yes	No	No	Fail	N/A	39	N/A	50	N/A
4	UZ080	Front	ABA	XTX3A-1	Zylon Hybrid	September-2001	45	4	Yes	Yes	Yes	Yes	Yes	Yes	Fail	N/A	N/A	N/A	N/A	N/A
5	UZ099	Back	ABA	XTX3A-1	Zylon Hybrid	October-2002	32	3	No	Yes	Yes	Yes	Yes	Yes	Fail	46	N/A	55	N/A	N/A
6	UZ046	Back	Point Blank	ZL6	Zylon Hybrid	#N/A	unknown	3	No	No	No	No	No	No	Pass	55	N/A	52	53	Fail
7	UZ053	Front	Point Blank	ZL6	Zylon Hybrid	#N/A	unknown	3	No	No	No	No	No	No	Pass	29	39	58	55	Fail
8	UZ070	Back	Point Blank	ZL6	Zylon Hybrid	#N/A	unknown	3	No	No	No	No	Yes	No	Pass	37	36	53	50	Fail
9	UZ079	Front	Point Blank	ZL6	Zylon Hybrid	#N/A	unknown	4	Yes	No	Yes	No	No	Yes	Fail	45	33	52	51	N/A
10	UZ098	Back	Point Blank	ZL6	Zylon Hybrid	#N/A	unknown	3	No	No	No	No	No	No	Pass	34	35			Fail

Notes:

1) The 9 mm threats for level IIA armor are a 124 gr. 9 mm FMJ RN bullet with a velocity of 1090 (+50/-0) ft/s for NIJ 0101.03 armor and a velocity of 1120 (±30) ft/s for NIJ 0101.04 armor.
2) The magnum threats for level IIA armor are a 158 gr. 357 Magnum JSP bullet at 1250 (+50/-0) ft/s for NIJ 0101.03 armor and a 180 gr. 40 S&W FMJ bullet at 1055 (±30) ft/s for NIJ 0101.04 armor.
3) The 9 mm threats for level II armor are a 124 gr. 9 mm FMJ RN bullet with a velocity of 1175 (+50/-0) ft/s for NIJ 0101.03 armor and a velocity of 1205 (±30) ft/s for NIJ 0101.04 armor.
4) The magnum threats for level II armor are a 158 gr. 357 Magnum JSP bullet with a velocity of 1395 (+50/-0) ft/s for NIJ 0101.03 armor and a velocity of 1430 (±30) ft/s for NIJ 0101.04 armor.
5) The 9 mm threats for level IIIA armor are a 124 gr. 9 mm FMJ RN bullet with a velocity of 1400 (+50/-0) ft/s for NIJ 0101.03 armor and a velocity of 1430 (±30) ft/s for NIJ 0101.04 armor.
6) The magnum threats for level IIIA armor are a 240 gr. 44 Mag LSWCGC bullet at 1400 (+50/-0) ft/s for NIJ 0101.03 armor and a 240 gr. 44 Mag SJHP bullet at 1430 (±30) ft/s for NIJ 0101.04 armor.
7) The armor condition refers to a visual inspection. Condition 1 refers to armor that shows no visible signs of wear and is in new or "like new" condition. Condition 2 refers to armor that shows light to moderate signs of wear. Condition 3 refers to armor that shows significant signs of wear (daily use for extended period). Condition 4 refers to armor that shows signs of extreme wear or abuse.

Appendix D. Individual Armor Models Tested

SCBA Tri-flex® Models

Production of this line of NIJ 0101.03-compliant armors was discontinued by SCBA in the spring of 2004. Fourteen of these armors were tested, including two that were more than five years old.

SCBA Tri-Flex® Models

Protection Level	Model Number	Number Tested
IIA	AZG-IIA 896280	1
II	AZG-II 995120	10
IIIA	AZG-IIIA 896280	3
	Total	14

- Twelve of the 14 Tri-flex® armors were penetrated by at least one round.

- Of those 12, 7 panels (50% of total panels tested) experienced penetrations from all six rounds and eleven of the 14 panels experienced four or more penetrations.

- One third of the 9mm rounds that did not penetrate the armor resulted in an excessive BFS and all armors experienced excessive BFS from the magnum rounds.

- The level IIA armor and the level II armors tested experienced at least two penetrations.

SCBA Ultima® Models

SCBA voluntarily stopped production of these models in the fall of 2003, and issued "Performance Pacs," upgrade kits that were intended to assure an armors performance as originally warranted. NIJ-sponsored tests in the fall of 2004 showed that the upgrade kits were insufficient, and SCBA has recently warned that all of these armors should be removed from service. Fifteen of the original ballistic armor panels were tested, including 10 that were greater than 60 months old.

SCBA Ultima® Models

Protection Level	Model Number	Number Tested
IIA	ZYL-IIA 898101	2
IIA	SMU-IIA+105130	1
II	ZYL-II 898101	7
II	SMU-II+001221	2
IIIA	ZYL-IIIA 898101	3
	Total	15

- Seven of the 15 (43%) Ultima® models tested experienced at least one penetration.

- Of the 8 Ultima® armors that did not experience a penetration, all experienced excessive BFS.

- Twelve of the fifteen armors experienced excessive BFS from both the 9 mm and other rounds.

Protective Products International

Protective Products International (PPI) model Z-22 are constructed entirely from woven Zylon®. Nine armors, collected from two law enforcement agencies, ranged from 47 to 50 months in age.

Protective Products International

Protection Level	Model Number	Number Tested
II	Z-22	9
	Total	9

- All nine armors tested experienced a penetration by at least one round.

- All of the BFS resulting from the other threat round exceeded 44 mm.

ABA Xtreme ZX Model

American Body Armor (ABA) reduced the warranty period of its level II ZX model XTZX2-1 (0101.04 compliant) from 60 months to 30 months in August 2004, in response to evidence that this and other ZX models were showing significant degradation in their ballistic performance. This hybrid armor model is constructed from laminated Zylon®, woven Zylon®, and ultra high molecular weight polyethylene.

American Body Armor ZX

Protection Level	Model Number	Number Tested
II	XTZX2-1	4
	Total	4

- All four armors tested experienced penetrations by at least two rounds.
    - Two of the penetrated armors were nearly four years old.
    - The age of one armor could not be determined.
    - One armor was two years old (within the modified warranty period).

ABA Xtreme X Models

These hybrid armor models are constructed from laminated Zylon®, woven Zylon®, ultra high molecular weight polyethylene, and aramid material.

American Body Armor X

Protection Level	Model Number	Number Tested
II	XTX2-1	4
IIIA	XTX3A-1	4
	Total	8

- Seven of the eight armors tested experienced penetrations by at least one round.

- The level IIIA armors experienced penetrations by two or more rounds and by both threats.

   o Two of these armors were penetrated by all six rounds.

- Two of the level II armors were penetrated by a single magnum round, and a third was penetrated by one magnum and one 9 mm round.

- Seven of the eight armors were less than four years old, and the age of the eighth armor could not be determined.

Point Blank Concealable Models

Eight Point Blank concealable armors were tested representing two models, ZL5 and ZL6 (levels II and IIIA, respectively, both 0101.04 compliant). These models are constructed from woven Zylon®, and aramid material.

Point Blank

Protection Level	Model Number	Number Tested
II	ZL5	3
IIIA	ZL6	5
	Total	8

- Three of the eight armors tested were penetrated by at least one round.

- One of the three level II armors was penetrated by multiple magnum rounds.

- Two of the five level IIIA armors were penetrated - one by a single 9 mm round, and one by three rounds, including both threats.

- All of the armors tested experienced excessive BFS, and six of the eight had BFS of 52 mm or greater.

- The age of these armors could not be determined.

Point Blank Tactical Model

Four Point Blank tactical armors were tested, all model F04-1. This level IIIA model (0101.03-compliant) was the only model with multiple samples tested that did not experience any penetrations. These armors are constructed with more layers of ballistic material than any other model tested, and had the smallest fraction of Zylon® material; less than 14 % of the total layers. These armors were constructed from woven Zylon®, aramid material, and ultra high molecular weight polyethylene.

Point Blank Tactical

Protection Level	Model Number	Number Tested
IIIA	F04-1	4
	Total	4

- None of the armors tested experienced any penetrations.

- Two of the four armors met the NIJ BFS criteria of 44 mm.

- The remaining two armors each had a single excessive magnum BFS (45 mm and 47 mm).

First Choice Armors

Eight First Choice armors were tested representing three models, the MF2000, MF733, and the MSF1IIA. The MF2000 is a NIJ 0101.03-compliant, level II armor, constructed entirely from woven Zylon®. The MF733 and MSF1IIA are NIJ 0101.04-compliant models designed for level IIIA and IIA threats, respectively. The MF733 is a hybrid, constructed of laminated Zylon®, woven Zylon®, and aramid material. The MSF1IIA is constructed from laminated and woven Zylon®. First Choice has indicated that as of June 2005, model MSF1IIA is no longer sold.

First Choice Armors

Protection Level	Model Number	Number Tested
IIA	MSF1IIA	1
II	MF2000	6
IIA	MF733	1
	Total	8

- Two of the six MF2000 armors experienced at least one penetration.

- All six MF2000 armors experienced excessive BFS from the magnum round. Five of the six experienced excessive BFS from the 9 mm round.

- The MSF1IIA and MF733 armors each experienced one penetration during testing, and each experienced at least one excessive BFS.

Gator Hawk Armors

Three Gator Hawk armors of the same model were tested. The GH-2-1023 is an NIJ 0101.04-compliant, level II armor constructed with woven Zylon® and aramid material.

Gator Hawk Armor

Protection Level	Model Number	Number Tested
II	GH-2-1023	3
	Total	3

- One of the three armors tested was penetrated by a single magnum round.

- All three armors tested experienced at least one BFS of 50 mm or greater.

PACA Armors

Two models of armor from Protective Apparel Corporation of America (PACA) were tested, the ZGII and the ZPG IIA (NIJ 0101.04-compliant, levels II and IIA, respectively). Both models are constructed from woven Zylon® and aramid material.

PACA Armor

Protection Level	Model Number	Number Tested
II	ZGII	1
IIIA	ZPG IIA	1
	Total	2

- The single ZGII armor tested was 18 months old. It experienced no penetrations, but experienced one excessive BFS.

- The single ZPG IIA armor tested was penetrated by three 9 mm rounds, and experienced two excessive BFS.

About the National Institute of Justice

NIJ is the research, development, and evaluation agency of the U.S. Department of Justice. NIJ's mission is to advance scientific research, development, and evaluation to enhance the administration of justice and public safety. NIJ's principal authorities are derived from the Omnibus Crime Control and Safe Streets Act of 1968, as amended (see 42 U.S.C. §§ 3721–3723), and Title II of the Homeland Security Act of 2002.

The NIJ Director is appointed by the President and confirmed by the Senate. The Director establishes the Institute's objectives, guided by the priorities of the Office of Justice Programs, the U.S. Department of Justice, and the needs of the field. The Institute actively solicits the views of criminal justice and other professionals and researchers to inform its search for the knowledge and tools to guide policy and practice.

Strategic Goals

NIJ has seven strategic goals grouped into three categories:

Creating relevant knowledge and tools

1. Partner with State and local practitioners and policymakers to identify social science research and technology needs.
2. Create scientific, relevant, and reliable knowledge—with a particular emphasis on terrorism, violent crime, drugs and crime, cost-effectiveness, and community-based efforts—to enhance the administration of justice and public safety.
3. Develop affordable and effective tools and technologies to enhance the administration of justice and public safety.

Dissemination

4. Disseminate relevant knowledge and information to practitioners and policymakers in an understandable, timely, and concise manner.
5. Act as an honest broker to identify the information, tools, and technologies that respond to the needs of stakeholders.

Agency management

6. Practice fairness and openness in the research and development process.
7. Ensure professionalism, excellence, accountability, cost-effectiveness, and integrity in the management and conduct of NIJ activities and programs.

Program Areas

In addressing these strategic challenges, the Institute is involved in the following program areas: crime control and prevention, including policing; drugs and crime; justice systems and offender behavior, including corrections; violence and victimization; communications and information technologies; critical incident response; investigative and forensic sciences, including DNA; less-than-lethal technologies; officer protection; education and training technologies; testing and standards; technology assistance to law enforcement and corrections agencies; field testing of promising programs; and international crime control.

In addition to sponsoring research and development and technology assistance, NIJ evaluates programs, policies, and technologies. NIJ communicates its research and evaluation findings through conferences and print and electronic media.

To find out more about the National Institute of Justice, please visit:

http://www.ojp.usdoj.gov/nij

or contact:

National Criminal Justice
 Reference Service
P.O. Box 6000
Rockville, MD 20849–6000
800–851–3420
e-mail: *askncjrs@ncjrs.org*